Responding to Child Abuse

Action and Planning for Teachers and Other Professionals

Dorit Braun

B S P

Bedford Square Press
in association with the
Community Education Development Centre

C E D C

Published by the
BEDFORD SQUARE PRESS of the
National Council for Voluntary Organisations
26 Bedford Square, London WC1B 3HU

in association with the
COMMUNITY EDUCATION DEVELOPMENT CENTRE
Briton Road, Coventry CV2 4LF

First published 1988

Typeset at Wordsmiths Typesetting, London

British Library Cataloguing in Publication Data

Braun, Dorit
Responding to child abuse: action and planning for teachers and other
professionals.
1. Children. Abuse by adults
I. Title
362.7'044

ISBN 0-7199-1241-5

Printed in Great Britain by Henry Ling Ltd., at the Dorset Press, Dorchester, Dorset.

Handbook edited, designed and produced by CEDC
Resources Unit, Briton Road, Coventry CV2 4LF.

Contents

1 Introduction and rationale 9

2 Users' guide 14

3 Setting the scene 19

Activity 1   Ice-breaker: hopes and needs 20
Activity 2   Ranking the causes of abuse 21
Activity 3   Interpreting the statistics 25
Activity 4   Definitions 29

4 Personal feelings and responses 31

Activity 5   Ice-breaker: unloading baggage 32
Activity 6   Identifying your secrets 33
Activity 7   Confronting feelings 35
Activity 8   Simulation: Cathy's story 39
Activity 9   Role plays on possible sexual abuse 45
Activity 10   Case studies 47

5 Reporting and referring 50

Activity 11   Visitors from relevant agencies 51
Activity 12   Signs and symptoms 54
Activity 13   Procedures 57

6 Sexuality 61

Activity 14   Images of sexuality 62
Activity 15   Likes and dislikes of one's own sex 63
Activity 16   The development of sexuality 64
Activity 17   Making definitions 65

7 Supporting 71

Activity 18   Sensitive listening 72
Activity 19   Sensitive responding 73

8 School and classroom ethos 75

Activity 20   Design an uncaring school 76
Activity 21   Activities to develop self esteem 77
Activity 22   Effective parenting? 79
Activity 23   Aims for a preventive curriculum 80

9 Children and adults 81

Activity 24   A caring adult 82
Activity 25   What is a family? 83
Activity 26   The needs of children 84
Activity 27   Viewpoints on childrearing 85
Activity 28   Crimes and punishments 86
Activity 29   Childhood memories 88

10 Resources 90

Understanding child abuse 90
Legal and policy issues 91
Training resources 91
Resources for personal, social and health education 92

■■■■■■■■■■■■■■■■■■■■■■■■■■■■■■■■■■■■■

This set of training materials has been designed to meet
the training needs of teachers and other professionals in
responding to issues raised by child abuse.

It has been tested in a number of local authorities in
both school-based settings and LEA-wide courses. Many
of the activities in this pack have also been found useful
for training with other professional groups, and for
working directly with parents. Courses can be therefore
designed from this handbook for a wide range of other
professional groups, with the minimum of adaptation.

■■■■■■■■■■■■■■■■■■■■■■■■■■■■■■■■■■■■■

This handbook was written by Dorit Braun, Development Officer, for the Family Education Unit of the national Community Education Development Centre (CEDC).

It is the result of ideas developed by a working party called together to assist the Family Education Unit in developing its ideas for training in this area. The working party was set up by Kate Torkington, in her former role of Assistant Director (Family Education) at CEDC. This group met over a year in order to devise, review and evaluate a range of training strategies which could form a training resource. Activities were then tested in a range of settings by staff from the Family Education Unit as well as by members of the working party. The other members of the working party were:

Gerry Bailey, Headteacher, Edgewick Primary School, Coventry, now Home School Training Officer, Family Education Unit, CEDC

Nancy Beacroft, Nottingham and Bassettlaw Health Education Unit

Bernard Clarke, Vice Principal, Burleigh Community College

Tricia David, Department of Education, University of Warwick

Susan Leyden, Adviser, Nottinghamshire

Mike Shire, Coventry Child Protection Team, NSPCC

Anne Shonveld, School Counsellor Burleigh Community College

Kate Torkington, Assistant Director of the Community Education Development Centre, now Head of Training, Department of Programme Development and Training, Bernard van Leer Foundation in the Netherlands.

Further ideas and activities were contributed by participants at a writing workshop organised by the Unit. The participants at the writing workshop were

Grace Cheese, Principal Educational Social Worker, Sutton Coldfield

Clifford Chew, Headteacher, Erdington Hall Junior & Infant School, Birmingham

Gill Combes, Central Birmingham Health Authority

John Lloyd, Education Support Service, Birmingham

Christine Owen, Deputy Head, Four Dwellings School, Birmingham

Chris Traxon, Staff Development Tutor, Birmingham Education Support Service

We are grateful to all of the above for their support and creative thinking.

We are also grateful to Peter Newell and the Children's Legal Centre for permission to include notes on confidentiality, from the document *Rights of the child,* to Mike Shire from the NSPCC who contributed three background papers to this handbook, and to *The Guardian*, Peter Beresford and Howard Sharron for permission to reproduce their articles.

Daphne Webb typed the many drafts with good humour and patience, and we want to thank her for her hard work and vital support.

Child abuse training for teachers

A great deal of attention is now being paid to issues raised by child abuse. Recent reports, enquiries and government circulars have all recognised the important role played by teachers in identifying instances of child abuse. Similarly, need for cooperation between the relevant agencies involved in child abuse has been recognised. Many reports have proposed that every school should designate one teacher to act as a liaison officer with social services departments on abuse cases.

This notion of the 'specialist teacher' should encourage greater cooperation between the agencies, but it is of limited value in aiding the detection and prevention of abuse. One major role played by teachers in child abuse cases is that of early identification of abuse, as a result of close everyday contact with children. The 'specialist teacher' might well improve the procedures of referral and liaison with other agencies, but he or she will still depend on the skills of the class teacher to recognise abuse.

It appears that teachers who do recognise abuse do so intuitively, for there is little or no initial or inservice training for teachers to help them develop such diagnostic skills. Nor is there training to help teachers take things further after the initial diagnosis.

Dealing with a child abuse case requires not only knowledge of local procedure and skills of referral. The teacher must also be able to come to terms with his or her own feelings about the abuse, in order to continue to work sensitively and effectively with the abused child and its family.

The other major training need for teachers is in the area of working with pupils to prevent child abuse. This is an issue which goes wider and deeper than child safety programmes. Teachers need to look at the ethos of their school, and of their classroom. They need to consider how child protection programmes fit into the social and personal education curriculum. They need to consider how the school can support parents, and what the aims of family/parenthood education should be.

Aims

The activities and materials contained in this handbook are designed to support training for professionals. Training using these activities will provide scope for:

Personal development, through opportunities to:

- examine the values and attitudes underlying concerns about child abuse
- identify personal values and attitudes to child abuse
- explore personal feelings about cases of abuse
- develop listening and responding skills
- examine critically definitions and checklists of signs of abuse
- explore one's own understanding and feelings about the nature of sexuality and its relationship to child sexual abuse.

Links with other agencies, through opportunities to:

- come to terms with local child abuse procedures and guidelines
- develop relationships with professionals working in relevant local agencies
- develop understanding of the work of relevant local agencies.

Development of curriculum responses by providing opportunities to:

- raise awareness of the need for whole school approaches to prevention and child protection programmes
- raise awareness of the need to involve parents, the community and other agencies in work on child protection
- raise awareness of the complex nature of family lifestyles in Britain today, in order to examine what aims are realistic for parenthood education programmes
- develop understanding and insight into the nature of adult/child relationships, in order to develop appropriate prevention and child protection programmes.

Such training might be provided by the 'specialist' teacher for colleagues within a school. Or it might be part of a local multi-agency training programme.

The activities in this handbook are neither exhaustive nor definitive. Our intention is that the materials should support trainers in working with professionals to look both at responding to abuse, and at longer-term ways it might be prevented. They should be seen as a bank of ideas to support training; a resource from which to select appropriate ideas and activities, not a book to work through from start to finish.

Although the materials aim to support training on issues of child abuse generally, there is more emphasis on child sexual abuse. This emphasis is in response to demands from the field – it is clear that it is this aspect of abuse which causes people the most concern. However, the range of activities included is sufficiently wide to support training which is not restricted to child sexual abuse.

It is important to clarify that this handbook presents a range of active learning exercises for use in a variety of training contexts. It does not present detailed information about either child abuse or recommended procedures. Such information is available from other sources, for example DES and DHSS circulars, and all trainers should be familiar with such information before running any courses. In addition, trainers planning to use this material need to have experienced a similar training process themselves in order that they will be familiar with that process and prepared for the issues which may arise.

The following section – *Users' guide* – gives suggestions for ways you might select from the activities. The Resources section gives details of additional resources which you may want to use in your training.

The training activities do not provide ideas for school lessons, although teachers will find that they can adapt many of the activities for use in school. Other professionals will also find that many of the activities can be adapted, and used to run parent support groups, as well as inter-agency courses on child abuse. The emphasis of these materials is on the development of awareness, insight and skill on the part of those professionals who deal with child abuse. This is

a necessary first step before the introduction of prevention programmes. We do present a range of ideas to support people in working out a prevention programme, but the detail of such a programme must be for professionals working together in a particular locality to sort out. Only they will know their patch, and only they will be in a position to work with members of the community to develop programmes in response to the specific needs of a community.

Responding to abuse

Most of the child abuse training currently on offer has focused on providing teachers with checklists of signs and symptoms of abuse and making sure they understand their legal responsibilities and are familiar with the local guidelines and procedures for handling cases of suspected abuse. While this information is relevant to teachers, its provision falls far short of their training needs.

In some ways the response to the issue of training teachers in this area has provided two contradictory messages:

▶ that teachers know nothing about abuse and have no skills in its identification – and so need to be given these; and

▶ that schools can introduce child safety programmes, and parent education programmes, and so aim to eliminate child abuse in the future by breaking the 'cycle of abuse'.

The first view underestimates the skills and experience of most teachers, while the second overrates the potential of schools to initiate social change.

Many teachers know intuitively if something is wrong with a child; very often the reason for not suspecting or reporting possible abuse is more to do with teachers' own feelings and worries than because they have not noticed that something is wrong. Teachers are frequently anxious about what may happen to a child following referral to social services, and are acutely aware of the complexity of deciding what are the best interests of a child.

Training needs to encourage teachers to trust their intuition about children. But it also needs to enable them to confront their feelings about abuse and abusers, and to recognise the ways these feelings might influence their actions. Values and attitudes need to be examined; teachers need to recognise that there are conflicting and contradictory explanations of why abuse occurs, and that these reflect value positions. Once they have identified their own value position they can be alert to whether and how it influences their reactions to cases of possible abuse.

The difficulty of training which focuses on signs and symptoms alone is that it does not confront feelings, attitudes and values. But these need to be explored before professionals can be ready to think about symptoms. Lists of signs and symptoms are also value-laden, and need to be debated and discussed. In cases of sexual abuse, the whole question of attitudes to sexuality will be raised, and will need to be explored.

Training for teachers also needs to consider the teachers' skills in dealing with a disclosure. If training simply informs teachers of their local child abuse procedure then it ignores the whole question of how they deal with the child and its family. Yet for teachers this question is of central concern, because they will need to maintain a relationship with the child and family after referring a case. Moreover, the procedures in operation in many authorities conflict with practice adopted by teachers for dealing with illness and behaviour difficulties where abuse is not suspected.

For instance in cases where abuse is not suspected a teacher will automatically discuss his or her worry with the child's parent. But in cases of suspected abuse, guidelines often state that parents should be 'informed' once the teacher has referred the case to social services or the NSPCC. In some areas the guidelines give different procedures depending on the kind of abuse suspected. In cases which are not at all clear cut this leaves the teacher in a considerable dilemma. These dilemmas need to be addressed in training: it is important to acknowledge the difficult personal and

professional decisions which need to be made, and to develop teachers' skills and confidence in making them. If these issues are not addressed in training courses, the result is often to make teachers feel impotent – they can feel that whatever they do will be wrong. It is vital that training should be constructive, and should leave teachers feeling better able to respond to cases of abuse.

We believe that teachers have some specific needs from training that may not be met from inter-professional training on child abuse. However, we strongly believe that professionals from the relevant agencies should be included in courses for teachers once the specific needs of teachers have been addressed. It is crucial that relationships are developed and perceptions shared, in order to facilitate cooperative working between the agencies to protect children.

Other professionals and parents

Moreover, the training needs of other professionals have considerable overlap with those of teachers. All workers involved in child abuse need opportunities to understand their own values and attitudes towards abuse, and to compare their own feelings about abuse and abusers. For this reason many of the training activities in this handbook are relevant to a wide range of professions, and training programmes can be devised for a wide range of professional groups involved in child care or services, with a minimum of adaptation.

Parents too are concerned about child protection, and many schools seek to actively involve parents in the personal and social education curriculum. Many of the activities in this handbook have been used by parent groups to raise their own awareness, and to think about how they can support the work of the school in this area.

Child protection programmes

A school curriculum which seeks to empower children, and enable them to develop personal qualities that could help to protect them from abuse now, and in the future, is much wider than simply telling children how to say 'No' to

▷

strangers. Activity 23 asks teachers to develop their own aims for the curriculum. The ideas discussed below were developed by the working party which helped develop this training handbook, using this activity.

▶ The curriculum would need to be delivered in a school with an ethos which empowers children, a school which allows them to voice ideas, opinions and feelings, treats them with respect, values their contributions, and treats their families as valued partners in the educational process.

▶ The curriculum would need to include work on

Families – breaking down stereotypes and myths of the so-called 'ideal' family.

Relationships – with families, friends and peers.

Personal identity – Who am I? How did I get to be the person I am? What influences me?

Human rights/children's rights – What are the basic rights of all human beings? Are children's rights any different?

Sexuality – the development of sexual awareness, our bodies, personal safety.

▶ Such a curriculum will be delivered in a number of contexts including health, education, personal and social education and language work. It will need to be co-ordinated to ensure its delivery to all pupils regardless of sex, age or ability.

This handbook does not attempt to cover all the ground that would need to be covered in such a 'proactive' curriculum. We only include dimensions that will not easily be found elsewhere. The central element of family life education can be developed using two Open University packs which contain a wide range of appropriate materials to support experiential approaches – *Family lifestyles* and *Childhood*. Details are given in the Resources section. Similarly there has been a lot of work to develop child safety schemes based on *Kidscape* and the Rolf Harris video *Kids can say no*. (Details are also given in the Resources section).

Less attention has been given to power relationships between adults and children, yet these are of central concern if we are to empower children, and enable adults to protect and support children. Nor has much attention been given in published teaching packs to the question of sexuality, and yet this must be dealt with if we are concerned with prevention of child sexual abuse. This handbook therefore contains ideas for the proactive curriculum around these dimensions. It does not attempt to duplicate other resources which already exist.

The introduction of preventive work in schools and communities is considerably more complex than many recent initiatives might lead us to think. Teaching children to say 'No' will not prevent child sexual abuse. It needs to be conveyed as part of a wider message of empowering children otherwise it will cause confusion and concern to parents, teachers and pupils.

Teachers need training and support to initiate appropriate prevention work. First, all schools and communities are different. For this reason all schools will need to adapt and revise any materials and ideas to their own situation. Second, the protection of children is linked to the way adults and children relate in general, and awareness to self awareness and self esteem in particular. We know that victims of abuse very often feel themselves to be guilty, and at fault in some way. A prevention programme needs to look at ways schools can enhance children's self esteem. And it also needs to deal with the way that adults can undermine children's sense of self worth. These questions relate to the organisation and structure of schools, as well as to classroom ethos, and to relationships with parents. Training needs to enable teachers to explore their perceptions of these issues, and to support them in introducing changes into schools.

Education for parenthood

A common panacea which, it is suggested, would break the 'cycle of abuse' is that of providing parenthood education. However, this is fraught with difficulty. There are no simple right and wrong ways to be a parent. Teaching parentcraft skills to teenagers who may be a long way from becoming a parent, or who may never become parents is not appropriate. Moreover, it is arguable whether such skills can actually be taught. Most parents will comment that nothing could have effectively prepared them for parenthood. Several studies have shown that parents feel that the most useful type of preparation would have been insight and understanding into the emotional side of family life – which is usually omitted from many courses except in the most superficial way. Although parenthood education cannot make people into good parents (whatever that might be), family education courses can explore the realities of family life, and encourage people to see that living in a family is not the dream world of media and advertising images. Training needs to enable teachers to explore what can be expected of parenthood and family life education courses, and to see how these can become part of a whole school approach to child protection.

Supporting parents

Moreover, given the realities of parenting in our society, once teachers are aware of the limits of education for parenthood, they can begin to think about the ways schools can support parents in their task. Schools can offer parent support groups, or drop-in facilities, or adult education opportunities. Again, the ways this support is offered will vary according to different localities, but it is important that it be considered in training courses which aim to develop prevention programmes.

Supporting pupils

Once pupils are working in a caring environment, and feel valued, it is appropriate to develop their skills of assertiveness and of coping, so that they might be better equipped to deal with difficult situations if these arise, or feel able to disclose if they so wish. There is a range of materials now available on the market

to suit this purpose, and we do not repeat these ideas here. The Resources section reviews the available materials, and in training courses it would be important to provide opportunities for teachers to review and adapt such materials for their own needs.

Childrearing practice

Last, but by no means least, prevention programmes need to take on board the issue of childrearing. Sometimes approaches to childrearing practices and discipline may involve relationships where the adults' power over their children renders those children unable to disclose abuse, or even to know that they are not to blame for abuse. This will throw up a range of cultural factors and beliefs about childrearing, and will also involve people in reliving experiences, perhaps painful ones, from their own childhood. They may have experienced abuse themselves, as an adult or as a child. Although we feel such issues are central to the long term prevention of child abuse, we also feel that they should only be tackled by an experienced trainer, and even then the trainer should be working with a group which has a high level of trust, and where confidentiality can be guaranteed.

Conclusion

Finally, it is important to recognise the limits of what schools can do. It is naive to think that schools can prevent child abuse occurring in the future, particularly as we do not fully understand why it occurs. We do know that it occurs in the context of a complex web of social and personal factors. Schools cannot change society; indeed the amount of time we spend at school is very limited in the context of our whole lives. So whilst we need to train and support teachers to respond to issues of child abuse we should not expect the problem to go away as a result. That requires more far reaching social and political changes.

2 Users' guide

You will need to put some time and effort into planning to use these materials. Training in child abuse is demanding, difficult and sensitive, and the trainer should expect to think carefully about the needs of the group being trained.

The activities which follow can be used to form the basis of a wide range of training courses for teachers and other professionals, as well as for parents. You will need to select activities according to the needs and interests of your group, the aims of your course, and the time you have available. You will find it helpful to read the introductions to each section, where each activity is outlined in brief, with suggestions about how you might select activities for your group.

The agencies involved with child abuse will vary in different localities, and procedures will also vary. It will be important that you familiarise yourself with local conditions and relationships before running any training courses in child abuse. You should also read the relevant national and local guidelines. You may want to ensure that they have been read by your course participants in advance of any training.

Working with groups

For group work in the area of child abuse, group leaders will need to ensure that they design a course which will:

- build group trust and support
- encourage participants to examine their own attitudes, values and feelings
- develop participants' understanding of issues of procedure, signs and symptoms, and of preventive work.

Such courses require two trainers, at least one of whom is female, in order to provide mutual support and to ensure sensitivity to the needs of individuals in the group.

The trainers will need to be skilled in working with groups, and in the use of experiential learning techniques. In particular, you should have thought through how you will handle different views in a group, some of which you may find personally objectionable. You will also need to have had some preperation or training in the issues of child abuse.

Disclosure in a group

Trainers should be prepared for the fact that some participants in groups may disclose instances of child abuse that they have suffered. Sometimes they will be disclosed in a pair or small group; sometimes in a plenary session . Sometimes participants may themselves have forgotten about the incident or incidents until discussion triggers off memories. You will need to have thought about how you will respond to such disclosures, and to have discussed this with your co-trainer.

It will also be vital to develop a group which is supportive. There are likely to be occasions where a disclosure is made in pairs or small groups and where you do not know about it. Group members will need to support each other, and there are activities in the handbook which are designed to help this group support develop at an early stage.

Make sure you are available during coffee breaks and at the end of course sessions to support people should they wish it. However, note that people may well prefer to get support from a close friend or partner. You may find it helpful to have a list of agencies in your area to whom you can refer individuals who may want more specialist counselling.

It is important to remember that people will choose whether or not to disclose, and to whom they disclose. It is also important to recognise that many things can trigger off memories – a book, television programme, newspaper article – and not just an activity which you include in your course.

Selecting from the activities

In order to design a course based on this handbook we recommend that:

1 You select activities throughout the course that enable group trust to be developed, and enable individuals in the group to feel valued and supported. A number of activities included in this book can be used for this purpose.

2 You should use at least one activity from Section 3, *Setting the scene*, in the first session of your course. These activities will enable participants to examine their own values and attitudes. They will also introduce some of the issues for debate and discussion in the rest of the course. However, note that these activities demand a high level of literacy, so you may need to adapt them to suit your group.

3 Once you feel confident of the development of the group we recommend that you introduce at

least one activity from Section 4, to enable participants to explore their feelings about abuse.

4 We strongly recommend that work on procedures and on signs and symptoms is tackled only after group members have examined their attitudes, values and feelings about child abuse. They will need to be aware of their own value positions before they can make informed judgements about signs and symptoms.

5 We further recommend that when you do embark on work on procedures you invite professionals from the relevant agencies – police, social services, educational social workers, educational psychologists, health visitors, NSPCC, and paediatricians – to join your course meetings. Ideas for ways they can be invited in are given in Section 5 *Reporting and referring*.

6 On a course which is longer than one day, we suggest that you plan only the detail of the first one or two meetings, and leave enough flexibility in your plans for following meetings to ensure that you can respond to the needs and interests of your participants.

These materials are intended as a flexible resource to support training. Overleaf, we present brief course outlines which give a flavour of the variety of courses which can be run based on this handbook. You should also refer to the Resources section, which gives details of additional materials which you may wish to include in your course.

Course outlines

A course for primary headteachers on child abuse

Three 2 hour evening meetings.

Aim: to raise awareness of the teacher's responsibilities for detection and referral.

Pre-course reading: LEA guidelines and procedures for child abuse.

First meeting: values and attitudes

Introductions – the aims of the course; course leaders; course participants.

Activity 1 Ice-breaker: hopes and needs – share previous experience of child abuse cases, and discuss hopes and needs from this course.

Activity 2 Ranking the causes of abuse – explore values and attitudes about abuse; work cooperatively; develop the group.

Second meeting: personal responses

Activity 5 Ice-breaker: unloading baggage – warm up, develop the group, clear people's minds.

Activity 7 Confronting feelings – explore the personal feelings raised by cases of abuse.

Activity 9 Role plays on possible sexual abuse – explore the ambiguity of signs and symptoms; consider the teachers' responsibilities; discuss the involvement of other agencies.

Third meeting: referring

Activity 11 Visitors from relevant agencies – develop relationships with local professionals from relevant agencies, explore issues and dilemmas of referral of cases; discuss ways of liaising and cooperating informally on cases where abuse is suspected.

Course evaluation – things learned and further training needs.

A course for teachers on child sexual abuse

Six 3 hour meetings.

Aim: support the development of prevention programmes in schools.

First meeting: what is sexual abuse?

Introductions – the course aims, leaders and participants.

Activity 1 Ice-breaker: hopes and needs – identify expectations of the course, to aid course planning and evaluation.

Activity 3 Interpreting the statistics – critically examine the 'facts', discuss what it is we are trying to prevent, raise awareness of value positions underlying the 'facts', explore own value positions, develop the group, work cooperatively.

Activity 10 Case-studies – explore borderline issues of what group members feel does and does not constitute sexual abuse, examine personal feelings about abuse and consider how these influence ideas about and attitudes to prevention.

Second meeting: sexuality

Activity 5 Ice-breaker: unloading baggage – warm up, clear people's minds, develop group trust.

Activity 14 Images of sexuality – explore values and attitudes towards sexuality in our society, and the relationship of these to prevention programmes.

Activity 15 Likes and dislikes of one's own sex – explore attitudes and assumptions about sex and gender, map the terrain for the following discussion of sexuality in our society.

Activity 16 The development of sexuality – raise awareness of the idea of 'normal' sexual development.

Closing round: how I feel now ....

Third meeting: school responses

Activity 20 Design an uncaring school – warm up, raise awareness of the context for preventive work, create an agenda for change.

Activity 22 Effective parenting? – develop awareness and understanding of the need to support and involve parents in prevention programmes.

Activity 23 Aims for a preventive curriculum – consider aims for prevention work to be included in the curriculum, and raise awareness of the importance of cross curricula, whole school approaches.

Review materials – selection from Section 9 of this handbook and some of those recommended the Resources section.

Closing activity – possibilities for action in my school, and further needs for training and support from this course.

Fourth, fifth and sixth meetings

These meetings should support participants in trying out approaches in their own schools – they will therefore need to be planned after session three, so that they can respond to the needs and aims identified by participants.

An inter-agency course

A one day workshop.

Aim: to develop understanding of the roles and responsibilities of the relevant local agencies for child protection.

Course members include teacher, education social worker, educational psychologist, health visitor, social worker, police officer, paediatrician, all working in the same patch.

Introductions – the course aims, leaders and participants.

Activity 1 Ice-breaker: hopes and needs – of the course.

Activity 2 Ranking the causes of abuse – raise awareness of values and attitudes, explore own values.

Activity 6 Identifying your secrets – raise awareness of the difficulty of personal disclosure.

Activity 8 Simulation: Cathy's story – develop empathy with abused young woman, and with teacher hearing disclosure, raise debate about feelings and responsibilities for child protection being age and gender related, raise dilemmas about the use of local procedures and guidelines.

Activity 10 Case-studies – explore feelings about what does and does not constitute abuse.

Activity 12 Signs and symptoms – develop insight and understanding of the complexity of any individual case of child abuse; debate the value positions underlying signs and symptoms; discuss varying professional perceptions of and responses to signs and symptoms of abuse.

Evaluation and further training needs.

▷

An inter-agency course based at a school

A one day workshop, with the possibility of further follow up meetings.

For staff, parents, childminders, foster parents, social workers, health workers, and workers from other local agencies.

Aims: to examine roles and responsibilities in the detection of abuse; to set up prevention programmes.

Introductions – aims for the day, course leaders and participants.

Activity 25 What is a family? – examine values, attitudes and stereotypes about family life; break down barriers between staff and parents; establish that each individual on the course has something to offer; develop the group.

Activity 26 The needs of children – develop group trust, share insights and understandings about children's needs and entitlements, raise awareness of the limitations of school; raise awareness of the terrain to be covered in looking at child abuse.

Activity 9 Role plays on possible sexual abuse – to highlight ambiguities of some cases of abuse; explore peoples' feelings about abuse; and develop insight into the perceptions of the different professionals and of the parents.

Activity 13 Procedures – discuss the ways cases may be dealt with in the locality and explore perceptions about this.

Activity 20 Design an uncaring school – raise awareness of the school context for prevention programmes, and set an agenda for change.

Adaptation of Activity 23 Aims for prevention in our school and community – reach agreement on the aims for prevention by taking into account the perspectives of the whole group, enable future plans to be made.

Plans – for action, and for future meetings.

A school based day workshop

Aims: explore teachers' responsibilities and feelings about abuse and to develop a school policy.

Activity 5 Ice-breaker: unloading baggage – warm up and clear minds for the day, develop group trust.

Activity 2 Ranking the causes of abuse – explore values and attitudes about abuse, work cooperatively, develop the group.

Activity 4 Definitions – examine existing knowledge, values and assumptions, examine official definitions.

Activity 7 Confronting feelings – explore personal feelings raised by cases of abuse. Move discussion on to consider the teacher's response to each disclosure.

Plenary session – implications for school policy; ways forward.

A short workshop for parents on child abuse

One 2 hour meeting

Aim: to raise awareness of the significance of adult-child relationships in the context of parental concern for child safety. The workshop should be run with a group who have already worked together for a time.

Activity 26 The needs of children – raise awareness of the child in us, and use memories to construct ideas about children's needs.

Activity 28 Crimes and punishments – debate the appropriateness of certain forms of discipline and consider childrearing approaches and attitudes.

Activity 24 A caring adult – draw together ideas developed in the previous activities and consider the qualities in adults most valued by (children.

3 Setting the scene

These activities and stimulus materials encourage groups to explore their values and attitudes in relation to child abuse. It is vital that teachers, and other professionals, have an opportunity to do this before embarking on further training, or analysis of the detection and referral of abused children. All professionals need first to understand and come to terms with their own values about the causes of abuse. They need to appreciate that there are a range of attitudes underlying views about causes, and to recognise the values that underpin their own attitudes. They need, therefore, to discuss the lack of clarity or common agreement over what constitutes child abuse and why it occurs.

These activities also set the scene in terms of the development of the group. They encourage participants to work cooperatively, to value the contributions made by each member of the group, to see that there are no rights or wrongs, so that everyone has something relevant to offer, and so to develop trust and confidence in one another. Again, this is a vital first step in any course which is concerned with such a sensitive and potentially painful subject.

Ice-breaker: hopes and needs from the course

The ice-breaker helps people explore their hopes and needs from a course dealing with child abuse. You might wish to use an alternative exercise for the same purpose. There follow two activities which explore values about causes of abuse. The final activity in this section looks at definitions of abuse and is an important ingredient of any course.

Ranking the causes of abuse

This ranking exercise can be used to enable participants to identify their own values, to recognise and to debate the range of values and attitudes which exist in the group, and to acknowledge contrasting explanations of child abuse.

Interpreting the statistics

Many statistics have been offered to support the argument that we, as a society, should do more to protect children. We seldom examine the statistics to see what they are really telling us and what they are unable to tell us. The third activity explores the statistics of child abuse, and can be used to examine critically the myths and realities contained in the statistics, as well as to highlight the lack of common understanding over what constitutes abuse. The activity also encourages participation to explore the politics of child abuse, by examining how different groups and agencies interpret the same statistical information to suit their own purposes and objectives.

Definitions

The 'official' definitions of child abuse from government and local authority departments can seem shocking and alarming to people who are expected to respond to these definitions as part of their jobs. They often sound legalistic, detached and cold. The final activity in this section concerns definitions of child abuse. In this exercise participants construct their own definitions of abuse before looking at definitions made by official bodies. This enables them to examine their existing knowledge, values and assumptions, and to be aware of how these influence their reading of other people's definitions.

Ice-breaker: hopes and needs

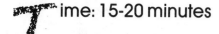ime: 15-20 minutes

Purpose

- Develop atmosphere of trust and support
- Reflect on previous experiences and consider the implications of these for training needs

Task

Ask participants to work in pairs, and to share any professional experiences they have had with child abuse.

Then ask the pairs to look back to when they, professionally, first met a case of child abuse. If they have had no experience, ask them to think in the present.

Ask them to discuss what caused most unease (or what they think would cause most unease).

▶ lack of general knowledge about such cases
▶ lack of general knowledge about procedure
▶ their feelings about such cases.

Ask them to rank these causes in order of priority.

Call the group back together and ask for feedback from the task.

Then ask participants to describe their hopes and needs from this course. Note these on a flip chart. You may need to identify those hopes and needs which cannot be met by your course.

Keep the flip chart notes to aid evaluation at the end of the course, or to aid planning future sessions of the course.

Ranking the causes of abuse

Time: 40-50 minutes

Purpose

- To examine the various explanations of why child abuse occurs and clarify one's own values in relation to these explanations
- To exchange ideas and consider alternative value positions of other course participants
- To emphasise that there is no common agreement on causes of child abuse
- To develop a climate where differences of opinion are valued and respected

Preparation

You will need to provide participants with sets of the statements provided on the following page. You will need one set for each pair. Each statement should be on a separate slip of paper.

Task

Ask participants to work in pairs. Give each pair a set of the statements, and ask them to rank the statements according to the ones they find most convincing as explanations of child abuse.

You will need to explain that the statements are deliberately complex in order to encourage debate and disagreement and to allow individual s to clarify their own ideas. You should suggest that participants use a diamond shape to rank the statements, in order to facilitate grouping the issues. But tell participants that it is quite alright to abandon the diamond if it hampers their discussion; they can use whatever system they prefer to rank the statements.

```
                1st
        2nd             2nd
    3rd         3rd             3rd
        4th             4th
                last
```

Allow around 20 minutes for this stage. Then ask pairs to join with another pair to compare and contrast their rankings. Allow around 10 minutes for this. Call all the participants together and ask each group of four to report which items they ranked top and bottom. Note these on a flip chart. Once all the results are on the flip chart ask for comments about the position given to each statement. Encourage discussion and debate.

Points you may want to highlight in discussion:

▶ There is no common agreement.
▶ People's rank order depends on personal values and experiences but these personal values influence our response to abuse so it is important to be aware of them.
▶ There are no easy panaceas – like preparation for parenthood – but what/who is a good parent? And just how much can school influence anyway?
▶ What aspects of parenting can be taught? You can if you wish use this exercise to negotiate the content and aims of the rest of your course.

You may prefer to devise your own statements. Alternatively you can use press cuttings, or photographs for the same exercise. It is important, though, to ensure that the items for ranking raise debate, and are not easy to accept or reject.

Further reading

The article which follows, which was originally published in *The Guardian* discusses the effect of poverty and social policy on child abuse and is also useful reading following the ranking exercise. Following discussion of the ranking exercise participants could read some of the literature on causes and explanations of child abuse. This is summed up well in the first part of the new Open University Pack, *Responding to child abuse and neglect*. A short readable paper, *Child abuse* which discusses the social factors involved has been produced by the Trades Unions' Child Care project. Other views can be found in *Understanding child abuse* by Jones et al, and *The politics of child abuse* by Parton. Details of all of these books are in the Resources section.

Statements for ranking

Unrealistic expectations

Mothers who abuse children are likely to have had babies for the wrong reason. They are desperately seeking affection, companionship and status. Children also get them council accommodation. The responsibilities of caring for babies prove too much for them and they resort to battering.

Social factors

Parents and social workers take the major blame for the problem of child abuse. Thus society is absolved of blame. Yet the life chances of many children are affected far more by a society which discriminates against them through differences in social class, education, housing and unemployment.

Family and cultural norms

Child abuse, far from being abnormal and pathological, arises from the interaction of culture, social organisation and social learning. Thus physical punishment is seen and experienced as normal by most family members and this is also true of incest in some families and communities.

Individual pathology

Only a few individuals, who are psychologically inadequate in some way, abuse their children. If we could clearly identify the particular social and psychological characteristics of these child abusers, we could predict children who will be at risk and take measures to ensure their safety.

A question of power

Child abuse is a simple matter of adults abusing the power they have over someone younger and weaker than themselves. The problem will only be solved if the rights of children are increased.

Day care provision

Small children make huge demands on their carers, especially if they are unsupported. It is all too easy to resort to violence to control children. Therefore if we want to prevent child abuse it is vital to develop daycare for children that is universally available.

Reconstituted families

Stepfathers are frequent abusers of the children in their care. Sadly, the demise of the traditional nuclear family means that increasing numbers of children are subject to the risks of belonging to a re-constituted family.

A violent society

Child abuse is just one aspect of the increased violence in society as a whole. The media must take a major responsibility for this because of its frequent portrayal of sex and violence.

Cycle of deprivation

People who have themselves been abused as children are more likely to abuse their own children. Such people need to be adequately prepared for the responsibility of parenthood in order to break the cycle of deprivation.

Pin the blame on poverty, not the parents

Nine years ago, the number of children in care in North Battersea, a deprived multi-racial inner city area in the London Borough of Wandsworth, was more than three times the national average. Local social workers initiated their own research project to find out why, including interviews with children in care, their parents, foster parents, social and care workers.

The findings revealed a disturbing lack of planning. Almost a third of children in care had no recorded initial plan. They were staying in institutions much longer than was originally expected, without clear or satisfactory reason and without adequate arrangements to ensure that decisions were actually made and reviewed. Plans often changed with social workers. Coordination between field and residential workers was poor. Parents and children seemed to have little say in either decision-making or the process of care. Research elsewhere revealed a similar picture.

Major changes followed in North Battersea. Planning was improved. A new emphasis was placed on involving parents and children wherever possible. In 1981, local social services were reorganised and social workers feel that this made it possible for them to work more effectively with other agencies and to get to know local people and their networks better. So, for example, instead of coming in cold to a crisis and taking children into care, they have been able to place them temporarily with family, friends and neighbours.

In 1982, the number of children in care in North Battersea started to decline, falling by near half by 1984. But two years ago this trend was reversed. The number of children coming into and remaining in care has risen appreciably and those seen to be at risk have now doubled. This coincides with worsening local social and economic conditions and echoes developments elsewhere.

The North Battersea findings add to the evidence linking poverty and reception into care. The overall picture is of families on desperately low incomes in the worst, cramped housing, with few supports or other resources. Over half are single parents and a growing number, rising to more than half, black

The poverty connection has particular importance because of the recent move to what is called 'permanency planning', which has been widely adopted by social service departments of all political colours, including Wandsworth. The emphasis is on permanency for the child, preferably with his or her own family, but failing that – within specific, and some have suggested, arbitrary time limits – with a foster or adoptive family.

Exhaustive efforts are supposed to be made to enable children to stay with their parents if possible but the whole emphasis of child care legislation and policy is on 'care' rather than prevention. Wandsworth is not unusual in devoting an increasing slice of social services resources to fostering and adoption while preventive work continues to be seriously underfunded.

As one North Battersea social worker said 'If children are in care, it's much easier for us to provide resources. Then you can get one hundred pounds for children's clothes . You'd have to fight a lot harder to get it for the child at home.'

If natural parents could be given the resources and support now made available to substitute families – who tend to be relatively better-off – they might more often be able to stay together. As another social worker put it, once a child has been removed from its natural parents, it may be seen as needing very special foster parents, although the natural family would have been expected to cope and judged inadequate if it couldn't.

While families with children in care may be stereotyped by a few terrible tragedies, the reality we encountered was very different. Most parents and children expressed positive and loving feelings for each other which care staff confirmed. Often they just didn't have the resources and support – human or material – to stay together. As one mother said, 'When they'd gone, I realised it was probably for the best, because at least that way they'd get three square meals a day.' Another made clear the cost of parenthood on her own: 'I try my best with my kids. When they were small they tangled my feet, and now they're grown they tangle my heart.'

Wandsworth, known as 'Mrs Thatcher's favourite borough' for its new-right policies, offers a worrying glimpse of future inner-city child care policy, as council estates are sold for upmarket redevelopment, care staff, day nursery and subsidised childminding places are reduced, and local amenities are run down. It raises the question of whether what we are seeing is a public policy of neglect rather than the parental failure we more often hear about.

The North Battersea research highlights two complex and crucial relationships: between social deprivation and reception into care, and between social work decision-making and resources. Both need to be better understood if child care policy is to improve and more children are not to be put at risk. The lesson from North Battersea is that while improvements in child care can be made, they may quickly be overtaken by the damaging effects of other policies.

More resourses are needed for housing, income maintenance, employment and day care provision to reduce family stress and insecurity. Supportive work with families could include family centres and proper payment to neighbours for short-term fostering.

Where children are seen as at risk or received into care, more emphasis must be placed on safeguarding both their and their parents' rights and involvement. And in view of the worsening situation facing many black families, improved training, resources and recruitment are needed to pursue more effective anti-racist child care. North Battersea offers a reminder that safeguarding child care is too big an issue to be left to social workers.

Peter Beresford
The Guardian July 8 1987

Interpreting the statistics

Purpose
- Raise awareness about the statistics on abuse
- Raise awareness about ways the statistics can be interpreted
- Develop understanding of the limitations of statistical information
- Develop insight into the politics of child abuse

Preparation

You will need copies of the current figures of child abuse provided on the following page. Alternatively, you can provide your own local statistics, or more recent national ones when these are available.

Task

Ask participants to work in groups of four to six people. Give each group a copy of the current figures of child abuse.

Ask each group to adopt one of the following 'perspectives' and carry out the specified task.

National Society for the Prevention of Cruelty to Children draft a press release based on these figures which you hope will substantially increase fund raising efforts.

Department of Health and Social Security draft a response to these figures which will not involve you in any additional expenditure.

Childline draft an advert for raising funds which makes use of the statistics presented here.

Department of Education and Science draft a statement for the press and local education authorities on the implications of these statistics for teachers, taking care not to involve the DES in any additional expenditure.

Local Education Authority draft a response to these statistics which will not involve you in any additional expenditure.

Professional group draft a letter to the local authority asking for their support to respond to the issues raised by these statistics.

Parent group draft a letter to your school asking for support, to respond to the issues raised by the statistics.

Allow groups 20-30 minutes to complete their task. Call a plenary session.

Debriefing

▶ Did participants think that their discussions and drafts were realistic?
▶ Why did the different actors involved use statistics in certain ways?
▶ What are the limitations of statistical information? What don't the statistics tell us?

Further reading

You may like to have available documents or press cuttings from the organisations included in the activity. Details of how to obtain the DHSS draft guidelines 'Working together', and addresses of other organisations are given in the Resources section.

You may also want to refer people to the readings listed at the end of the previous exercise, which cover different explanations of child abuse.

Interpreting the statistics

Statistics on child sexual assault

Child sexual assault is the sexual exploitation of a child who is not developmentally capable of understanding or resisting the contact, or the sexual exploitation of a child or adolescent who may be psychologically and socially dependent upon the perpetrator.

Child sexual assault takes many forms: exhibitionism and fondling, oral sex, sodomy, intercourse, and pornography.

Recent studies suggest that as many as one in three girls and one in five boys will experience some form of sexual assault before the age of eighteen.

In eighty-five percent of the cases, the offender is someone known to the child – a parent, relative, older friend or neighbour. In forty percent of all cases, the offender is a father figure. Three percent of all offenders are female.

In eighty-eight percent of reported cases, the child is subjected repeatedly to sexual assault. Because the child is persuaded to keep the activity a secret, it may continue undetected over a number of years.

The assault frequently occurs in the child's familiar surroundings, often in his or her own home or that of a relative or friend.

Source: Kidscape (details in the Resources section).

Parental situation by type of abuse (1977-1984)					
Parental situation	Physically injured	Failure to thrive	Sexual abuse	Neglect	Emotional abuse
Two natural parents	2665 (47)	127 (69)	91 (36)	100 (49)	24 (34)
Natural mother alone	1030 (18)	36 (19)	31 (12)	71 (35)	12 (17)
Natural mother & father substitute	1505 (26)	21 (11)	96 (38)	25 (12)	22 (31)
Natural father alone	178 (3)	1 (1)	17 (7)	4 (2)	2 (3)
Natural father & mother substitute	231 (4)		6 (2)		8 (11)
Other	102 (2)		9 (4)	4 (2)	2 (3)
Total	5711 (100)	185 (100)	250 (100)	204 (100)	70 (100)

Interpreting the statistics

Number of registered children by year and type of abuse

Year	Physical injury	Failure to thrive	Sexual abuse	Neglect	Emotional abuse	Other	Total
1977	689	27	7	na	na	277	1000
1978	715	26	8	na	na	323	1072
1979	683	17	8	3	na	366	1077
1980	774	15	11	15	na	301	1116
1981	807	30	27	30	4	291	1189
1982	661	21	40	44	17	295	1078
1983	672	15	51	62	31	281	1112
1984	707	34	98	50	18	209	1116
Total	5708	185	250	204	70	2343	8760
%	65	2	3	2	1	27	100

There were 8760 children placed on child abuse registers maintained by the NSPCC between 1977 and 1984. These figures include children in the same household, children thought to be at serious risk of abuse and children whose injuries were subsequently judged to have been caused accidentally. Figure 1 shows the number registered each year by the reason for registration. The majority (sixty-five per cent) of the registered children were physically injured. If we exclude the 'at risk' cases from the main analysis, ninety-five per cent of the children abused in 1980 were physically injured. This was the year prior to the widening of the register criteria to include other forms of abuse in addition to physical injury. By 1984 only seventy-eight percent of the abused children were physically injured. Among the other types of abuse, cases of sexual abuse have shown the greatest increase. They represented two per cent of the abused children in 1980, increasing to eleven percent in 1984.

Interpreting the statistics

Sex of the children

Significantly more boys than girls were registered for physical and emotional abuse, failure to thrive and neglect. Of the abused children fifty-four percent were boys. Among the sexually abused children the overwhelming majority (eighty-five percent) were girls. The age of the children also affected the sex distribution, particularly for the physically abused children. Boys aged between five and nine years and girls aged fourteen or over were more vulnerable. Of the physically abused five to nine year-olds, sixty-one percent were boys and sixty-seven percent of the children aged fifteen or more were girls.

Ages of children with different types of abuse (1977-1984)

Age	Physically injured	Failure to thrive	Sexual abuse	Neglect	Emotional abuse	National distribution†
0-4 years	3147 (55)	177 (96)	10 (4)	142 (70)	30 (43)	(28)
5-9 years	1325 (23)	6 (3)	67 (27)	41 (20)	23 (33)	(26)
10-14 years	1030 (18)	1 (0.5)	130 (52)	19 (9)	14 (20)	(32)
15-17 years	206 (4)	1 (0.5)	43 (17)	2 (1)	3 (4)	(14)
Total	5708 (100)	185 (100)	250 (100)	204 (100)	70 (100)	(100)
Mean age	5 years & 8 months	1 year & 7 months	11 years & 7 months	4 years & 1 month	6 years & 10 months	

†(Population estimates, 1984)

Source: S. Creighton 'Quantitative assessment of child abuse' (based on original data from the NSPCC's register of research) in P. Maher (ed) *Child abuse. The educational perspective.* Details in the Resources section.

Definitions

Time: 1 hour

Purpose

- Identify participants' own knowledge about child abuse
- Share the group's existing knowledge about child abuse
- Explore feelings and attitudes towards abuse and abusers
- Examine government definitions of child abuse

Preparation

You will need blank index cards or slips of paper: enough for five cards per person. You will also need copies of the 'official definitions' provided on the following page. The group will need to have explored their initial perceptions of the issues involved in child abuse, and be trusting and supportive before doing this task. Good preparatory activities are the *Hopes and needs ice-breaker* (Activity 1) and the *Ranking exercise* (Activity 2).

Task

Form groups of eight to ten people. Give each individual five blank index cards, or slips of paper.

Ask everyone to write a statement on each card. Each statement should be different and should contribute towards a definition of child abuse. Alternatively, ask them to complete the sentence, 'child abuse is ....' in five different ways.

Allow 15-20 minutes for this. The statements should then be collected together. The group should then decide how to distribute the cards so that each person selects three cards that they agree with, but did not write themselves. Individuals then tell the other group members which cards they chose, and why.

The group should then review the selected cards in order to write a collective definition of child abuse. Allow around 20 minutes for this. You can give the groups large sheets of paper and felt tip pens so that the definitions can be displayed. Call the groups together and ask each to present their definition. Encourage discussion and debate of the definitions.

Then hand out copies of the 'official definitions' given, or, alternatively, use the definitions found in your local guidelines.

Debriefing

Give people time to read the definitions, then ask for their reactions:

▶ How did they feel when they read them?

▶ How do these definitions compare with the definitions written by the group?

You may need to point out that the official definitions need to be legalistic because they are used together with legal processes.

You could also discuss the implications of this activity for the way people learn. Examining one's own knowledge is a vital first step in reviewing and evaluating new information and ways of seeing the world. This has obvious implications for teaching child protection in terms of the content of what is taught and the process by which it is taught.

Further reading

Two books which explore the complex feelings and emotions of child abuse can be recommended to participants at this point – *'The bone people'* by Keri Hulme, and *'Cry hard and swim'* by Jacqueline Spring.

Details are in the Resources section.

Definitions of child abuse

The definitions presented here broadly correspond to those used by the DHSS in their 1986 document *'Child abuse – working together'*.

Physical injury

Children under the age of seventeen where the nature of the physical injury is not consistent with the account of how it occurred; or where there is a definite knowledge or reasonable suspicion that a person having custody, charge, or care of the child, inflicted or knowingly did not prevent the injury. This includes children to whom it is suspected that poisonous substances have been administered.

Physical neglect

Children under the age of seventeen who have been persistently or severely neglected physically, to such an extent that their health and development are impaired. Particular attention is drawn to food, hygiene, warmth, clothing, supervision, stimulation, safety precautions and medical care. Serious inadequacies in these areas may constitute neglect.

Failure to thrive

Children under the age of seventeen who have been medically diagnosed as suffering from severe non-organic failure to thrive, for example hair loss, poor skin tone, circulatory disorders, significant lack of growth. Although more easily recognisable in younger children it also applies to older children.

Emotional abuse

Children under seventeen where there is a persistent coldness, hostility, or rejection by the parent or care-giver, to such an extent that the child's behaviour and development are impaired.

Sexual abuse *as defined (above)*

The involvement of dependent, developmentally immature children and young persons in sexual activities that they do not fully comprehend, to which they are unable to give informed consent, and which violate social and family taboos. Sexual abuse may also include exposure of children to sexual stimulation inappropriate to the child's age and level of development.

Potential abuse

Children in situations where they have not been abused but where social and medical assessments indicate a high degree of risk that they might be abused in the future, including situations where another child in the household has been harmed, or where the household contains a known abuser.

These categories of abuse are not necessarily exhaustive, nor are they mutually exclusive. All of them may result in failure of the child to thrive.

This section deals with the feelings that are aroused when abuse is suspected or disclosed. These feelings are both complex and ambiguous. Teachers and other professionals may feel angry or hurt on behalf of the child. They may feel 'out of their depth'. They may feel desperate to protect the child. They may feel desperate to deny that abuse is taking place at all. They may wish to control the information, and not to pass it on to the relevant local agencies.

All of these feelings need to be explored if teachers are to be able to protect children. It is crucial to include at least one activity from this section on any course for professionals. But feelings like these can only be explored in a supportive and trusting atmosphere. For this reason we feel that the activities in the previous section are a vital first stage.

Ice-breaker: unloading baggage

This activity will clear people's minds in order that they can examine the complex feelings aroused by child abuse.

Identifying your secrets

The next activity looks at the feelings aroused when we are asked to disclose personal information. It does not demand disclosure and is useful in making people aware of how difficult it is to disclose. It thus makes them aware of the need for sensitive listening and responding. Listening skills are developed in the activities in Section 7. You may also want to use this activity to raise awareness that it is vital to have come to terms with our own feelings about abuse, to be able to react appropriately to disclosure. However, your group may already be well aware of the need to examine their feelings in relation to abuse, and you could therefore decide not to use this activity.

Confronting feelings

This activity presents four detailed cases of child abuse, all written from the point of view of the child. It asks you to confront the feelings aroused by such descriptions. The activity raises questions about the motivation behind media interest in child abuse. The personal feelings aroused by this activity mean that it should only be done in a trusting atmosphere, and that there should be time for adequate debriefing.

Simulation: Cathy's story

The simulation provides an opportunity to come to terms with the feelings aroused by a detailed disclosure of sexual abuse. Cathy is a teenager, and the simulation encourages discussion of the way our feelings about the protection of children relate to their age. It also raises the legal and moral dilemmas associated with sexual abuse of teenage children. Further, it is an opportunity to develop empathy with the abused child, as well as with the teacher who hears her disclosure. The activity raises questions about local authority guidelines, and how they should be followed. This helps make people aware of the need to develop relationships with other relevant agencies before crises occur. Many issues and feelings should surface in discussion. Allow plenty of time for debriefing, and use the simulation only if you feel confident about leading the debrief.

Role plays on possible sexual abuse

The role plays are designed to highlight the ambiguity of signs and symptoms. They draw attention to the feelings aroused by professionals' responsibilities for detection of abuse. Such feelings will be personal and professional. Teachers and childcare workers, in particular, may need their confidence boosted to trust their instincts about whether a child is at risk. They are the only professionals who have long term relationships with a child and their family. They are also experienced in dealing with children who are, for example, unwell but not being abused. They will need time to discuss the uncertainties surrounding signs and symptoms, and their feelings about this.

Case studies

This activity could be used instead of the role plays if you or your group feel uncomfortable with role play. The case studies and the role play raise similar dilemmas: the borderline between what is and is not abuse; the point at which other agencies can be consulted; the point at which referral should be made; and the feelings associated with different levels and types of abuse.

Ice-breaker: unloading baggage

*T*ime: 10-15 minutes

*P*urpose

- Warm up
- Develop trust and support within a group
- Offload something to clear the mind for the work to be done in a course session

*T*ask

It is important to be seated in a circle for this exercise. Explain to participants that the activity will be a round, i.e. that each person will speak in turn. One of the course leaders should begin the round, to set the tone and level of disclosure. Ask participants to 'offload' something which has really irritated or annoyed them. Tell them to pretend to 'take it out of their pocket or bag, throw it into the middle of the table and only collect it again at the end of the course session'.

Participants may say 'pass' if they wish, but try to stick to the round – if necessary by passing round a piece of chalk and pretending it is a microphone, or a shopping bag in which to collect the 'unloaded baggage'.

Identifying your secrets

 ime: 20-30 minutes

 urpose

- Raise awareness of how difficult it can be to disclose personal information or feelings
- Raise awareness of the need for listening skills when a disclosure is made
- Raise awareness of the need to have come to terms with one's own feelings about abuse in order to respond sensitively to disclosures

reparation

You will need enough copies of the worksheet overleaf to provide each participant with a copy.

ask

Ask participants to work individually. Ask them to anticipate how threatened they would feel disclosing and discussing their behaviour on a one to one basis with a specific friend or acquaintance. Explain that threat involves the degree to which they would feel uncomfortable and/or be less esteemed as a result of their disclosure.

Individuals should complete the worksheet using the rating scales provided.

Allow around 5-10 minutes for this. Then call a plenary session and ask for feedback and comments. You can structure the plenary around two areas:

▶ things you have learnt about yourself

▶ implications for how we respond to child abuse

Variations

You could ask participants to do their ratings for both a close friend and a work colleague or acquaintance, to highlight that while some things are easier to disclose to someone you know, others may be easier to someone who is further removed from you. You could also ask participants to add two areas of their own to the list: one statement which they would not feel threatening to discuss and one which they would feel too threatening to discuss. This would ensure that everyone becomes aware of the items they feel unable to disclose to others.

Identifying your secrets

Think of a friend or acquaintance. How would you feel about discussing each of the items in the list below with that person? Use the following scale to give a rating to your feelings for each item.

5 Impossible; much too threatening
4 Very threatening
3 Moderately threatening
2 Slightly threatening
1 Not threatening at all

Areas	Your Rating
Family relationships	
Things that make you happy	
Your body	
Feelings about death	
Social relationships	
Use of leisure	
Sexual feelings and behaviour	
Feelings of depression	
Political preferences	
Intellectual capacity	
Homosexual tendencies	
Socioeconomic background	
Your work	
Things that make you angry	
Fear and anxieties	
Religious beliefs	

Allow 7 minutes for this. Then call a plenary session.

Confronting feelings

⏶ ime: 20-30 minutes

This activity can cause discomfort or distress and personal support should be available from group leaders and/or group members. The exercise should not be used before a supportive atmosphere has been developed.

urpose

- Identify one's own feelings about child abuse
- Consider how these feelings are age and gender related
- Consider how feelings about abuse affect professional action

reparation

For each participant you will need copies of the case histories on child abuse and the questionnaire.

ask

Participants should work individually – ask them to find a space to work in. Ask them to read each of the case histories on abuse of children and then complete the accompanying questionnaire which should help them identify their feelings. Make it clear that the questionnaire is for personal use and no aspects of it need be shared with the group. However, if you also complete the questionnaire and demonstrate your willingness to share, this is likely to encourage participants to share also. This will make the activity considerably more effective.

In the blank column of the questionnaire, participants should tick the items that come nearest to expressing their reactions at the time of reading the material. Omit any that were not honestly felt at the time.

Allow 7 minutes for this. Then call a plenary session.

Ask participants whether they wish to make interpretations about the results of the questionnaire (not necessarily their own results). What could responses indicate about peoples' feelings? Then ask if they wish to comment on any of the statements.

Debriefing

The group leader can direct attention to some of the statements. The following statements could initiate valuable discussion:

▶**Statement 9** Discussion pointers and interpretations. Normality of titillation from explicitly sexual material, even though it is concerned with child abuse.

▶**Statement 19** Need for more information (for example, where was mum in Case 3?) might indicate views on what is 'normal' sex.

▶**Statement 13** Issues of homosexuality and incest. Greek myths and legends and some more up to date theories suggest homosexuality and incest are part of our make up and that only socialisation suppresses them.

▶**Statement 21** Which case is worse and why?

▶**Statement 5** Refusing to believe may make us switch off from accepting evidence about abuse.

▶**Statements 10** and **12** Feelings of anger can motivate or restrict action.

▶**All statements** Conflicting emotions, like anger or pity, can paralyse, but being able to recognise them in oneself can be half the battle.

Some issues can be raised from the material itself, for example issues of female self image, and issues of teenage behaviour and responsibility.

You can ask the group how the picture they have built up of themselves from the questionnaire differs from what they thought they were like.

Ask participants to think back to Activity 2, *Ranking the causes of abuse* (if it was done at a previous session). Learning from the exercise they have just done, how do they now view child abuse – a crime, a personal problem, a social problem, a disease?

▷

Follow up

Ask participants to imagine that they are a form tutor in a school (or in a similar position of responsibility, for example, a children's centre leader or youth leader) to whom a child has just disclosed one of the case histories.

Ask them to work in small groups and allocate each group one case-study. Using the checklist below, ask the groups to consider their reactions to the disclosure.

Discussion checklist

1 Look at the case-study
How do you handle that disclosure?

▶ what do you say to the young person
▶ what should you avoid saying?

2 Look at procedures from the point of view of a tutor. Plot a flow diagram to show the different actions that could be taken.

3 What worries do you have about the various actions?

4 What are the implications for the school?

Allow around 20-30 minutes. Call a plenary session and ask for feedback on each of the points discussed.

You may like to hand out the checklist of 'Five things to tell a child who confides in you' to sum up some of the discussion.

Five things to tell a child who decides to confide in you

1 'I believe you'
2 'It's not your fault' (A child can never be held responsible for abuse received at the hands of others)
3 'I'm glad you told me'
4 'I'm sorry this has happened to you'
5 'I'm going to help you'

Further reading

We recommend reading *The bone people* by Keri Hulme, a novel which explores the complex feelings of adults and children in relation to physical abuse.

The Family Rights Group has produced papers which eloquently state parents' perspectives on abuse cases. Details are given in the Resources section.

Case histories

1

"I've never got on with my father. He's always preferred my sister. Every so often it all blows up and we have large rows, usually it's about him saying I haven't done my share of jobs in the house, or my room's a mess. My sister can get away with all that. The other night he came up to my room. He'd been drinking all night. There was some stuff on the floor – he just knocked me across the room. I hit my head on the cupboard, and bruised my shoulder and arm. And last week because I'd come in with my trainers on and got mud on the hall carpet he hit me across my face and head. Mum sometimes tries to stop him but I think she's scared of him. I don't want you to tell this to anyone – it'll just cause more trouble."

2

"I've always felt the odd one out in my family – mum said that the reason dad left was because they were always rowing about me. I was the ugly one – the clumsy one. Simon was the one who always got the good report .... one year my report was so bad I wasn't allowed to go on holiday and had to stay with my Grandma. I don't speak to anyone at home anymore – I just go home and sit in my room .... sometime I wish I hadn't been born at all."

3

"I never liked it, but I didn't know what to do about it. It started when my mum got a Saturday morning job. I suppose it was my fault because I just used to lie in bed and not get up. My dad would come in. One morning I woke up and found my dad in bed with me. I realised I was being touched and started pulling away. And then I realised it was my father touching my vagina and I continued to pull away. He told me that I should not kid myself because when I was asleep I was enjoying it. He said that I had been making sounds in my sleep that indicated how much I was enjoying his touching me, moaning and so forth. He spoke in a whisper, so he wouldn't wake the others. I didn't know what was going on, so I tried to relax and allowed him to continue."

"After the first time there would be frequent contact whenever anybody wasn't looking. If I was alone with him, or even with the whole family around, he would touch me or he would reach over to kiss me good-bye and French-kiss me instead."

"This was the closest thing I had ever experienced to love because I really did feel unloved. The only physical affection that I remember were the incidents with my father."

4

"I'm glad my mum's got a boyfriend, but I wish I wasn't left in charge so often. My mum works, so I have to collect my brothers from school, make their tea and look after them till she gets in. Most weekends she goes to stay with her boyfriend in Birmingham. Sometimes she forgets to leave money to buy food and there's nothing in the house to eat. Last weekend the littlest one was sick all night and I didn't know what to do. I'm always getting into trouble for missing lessons, but I just feel so tired and dizzy and I can't concentrate."

Questionnaire

Case study	1	2	3	4
1 I felt unable/reluctant to carry out the instruction to read the material.	☑	☐	☐	☐
2 I felt anxious (or fearful, or tense, or reluctant) when I first read the material.	☑	☐	☐	☐
3 I felt quite detached and read the material with clinical objectivity.	☑	☐	☐	☐
4 I was horrified (appalled/shocked) by the material.	☐	☑	☐	☐
5 I had difficulty in comprehending (or believing) that what happened could really be done knowingly by human beings.	☑	☐	☐	☐
6 I experienced feelings of physical nausea (or sickness, or faintness, or shock).	☑	☐	☐	☐
7 I felt guilty, as though in some way personally responsible or involved.	☐	☑	☑	☐
8 I felt deep sorrow (or I wanted to cry).	☐	☐	☑	☐
9 I felt some degree of sexual titillation.	☑	☐	☐	☐
10 I felt angry with the parents who sexually abuse their children.	☐	☐	☐	☑
11 I felt pity (or distress, or concern) for the child.	☐	☐	☐	☑
12 I felt angry with a society in which such things can happen.	☐	☐	☐	☑
13 I felt disturbed at the thought that I myself might be capable of such an act.	☑	☐	☐	☐
14 I felt pity (or distress, or concern) for the abusing adult.	☑	☐	☐	☐
15 I felt that such crimes should not go unpunished.	☐	☐	☐	☑
16 I felt sympathy, or concern, for the workers handling such a case.	☐	☑	☐	☐
17 I felt a need to be involved in some action to help similarly abused children.	☐	☑	☐	☐
18 I felt useless and incapable of reacting constructively.	☐	☑	☐	☐
19 I felt a strong need for more information about the circumstances of these cases.	☐	☐	☑	☐
20 I felt ashamed that such things can be done by human beings.	☐	☐	☐	☑
21 I felt that some forms of incest are worse than others and you can't lump them altogether.	☑	☐	☐	☐

Simulation: Cathy's story

Time: 1 hour at least

This activity should only be tried once an atmosphere of trust and support has been established. It is important to allow plenty of time for debriefing. If you feel unsure about leading and debriefing this simulation do not attempt it. This exercise may prompt participants to disclose instances of abuse. You should make sure that you are available during and at the end of the session to offer support if it is wanted.

Participants will need to be 'warmed up' to take part in the simulation – you could use some of the activities in Section 7 for this.

Purpose

- Develop empathy with an abused person
- Develop empathy with a person to whom abuse is disclosed
- Debate how feelings about sexual abuse relate to age and gender
- Debate legal and moral issues arising from such cases
- Raise awareness of the need to develop good relationships with local agencies involved in child protection

Preparation

You will need to have sufficient copies of the role briefs: the person playing Cathy will need both parts. The person playing the teacher, and the observer will need part 1 only. The observer will also need his or her instructions.

You will also need large sheets of paper and felt tip pens.

Task

1 Participants should work in threes. Ask them to find a space to work in and allocate roles of teacher, Cathy and observer. Then hand out the role briefs as appropriate.

2 Ask participants to begin the role play when they are ready. They should enact the scene which takes place in the toilet. They have around 7-10 minutes to do this.

3 Ask the observers to lead the debriefing by following their debriefing instructions. Allow 20-30 minutes for this.

4 Call a plenary session and form three groups:
– those who played Cathy
– those who played the teacher
– the observers

Give each group large sheets of paper and felt tip pens and ask them to note down all the issues raised for them by the simulation. Allow around 10 minutes. Ask each group to appoint a spokesperson, and call a final plenary session for the groups to report back to one another.

Debriefing

You will need to ensure that the following issues are raised in the final plenary session. They are likely to arise out of the feedback, but may need prompting:

▸ Did all the simulations result in a referral to social services? If not, why not?

▸ Did anyone make informal contact with other agencies, for example educational social workers?

▸ What difference would it have made if Cathy was thirteen? or sixteen?

▸ Did anyone offer contraceptive advice?

▸ What difference would it have made if Paul had been Cathy's mum's boyfriend and not her husband?

▸ What are the implications for teaching family issues and sex education in schools?

▸ What are the implications for the teacher's and school's role in detection and referral?

▷

Follow up

Ask participants to design a similar simulation exercise, but this time based on the sexual abuse of a boy. They should work in small groups and compare simulations after allowing time for the development of their ideas. (At least 30 minutes).

The purpose of this follow up is not to produce further training materials, but to focus participants' thinking on the complexity of feelings and issues surrounding the sexual abuse of boys.

In the debriefing for this follow up you will need to be alert to the following issues and questions:
Denial some participants may have decided that boys are never sexually abused
Age what difference does the age of a boy make to people's interpretations of abuse? Are there gender differences?

Power did people feel that boys should have been able to 'fight off' the abuser?
Homosexuality some participants may find the sexual relationships between Cathy and her stepfather understandable, but may think of a homosexual relationship as 'perverted'.

Further reading

The Children's Legal Centre has produced a leaflet, *Rights of the Child* on children's rights in child abuse cases. This includes a section on confidentiality which we reproduce on the following pages. This extract presents the child's perspective on disclosure and will be important reading for all professionals. You may want to spend time in a course session reading the extract and using it as a prompt for a discussion on the 'best interests of the child'.

Cathy's story

Observer's notes

Observing the simulation

Look for non-verbal cues to indicate the feelings of both 'actors'

Think about the way the 'teacher' is handling the disclosure

▶ How does this make 'Cathy' react?
▶ What are the implications for school procedure? For example, is confidentiality an issue?

Debriefing

1 Ask 'Cathy' how she feels about the way her disclosure was handled.
2 Ask her 'teacher' how she felt about the disclosure and about the way she handled it.

3 Make any comments or observations.
4 What issues have been raised for you all by this simulation about:
   ▶ abused children
   ▶ the teachers' role
   ▶ your local procedures
   ▶ personal and social education in secondary schools
   ▶ other issues.

Note

In debriefing this exercise you may discover that some or all of you in the group have yourselves experienced sexual abuse. You can ask one of the group leaders for support if you wish, or you may be able to support each other in your group of three.

Cathy's story

Briefing for role play

Part 1

Cathy, aged fifteen, has been in a personal and social education lesson where the discussion has been about sexual behaviour and contraception. In the midst of the discussion, Cathy bursts into tears and rushes out of the room.

After the lesson, the teacher finds her in the girls' toilets crying and asks her what is wrong.

Part 2

Cathy lives with her mum and stepdad, Paul, and two younger brothers, aged three and five years. She doesn't see her real dad at all; her parents separated when she was small. Her mum married Paul when Cathy was nine. At first things went well and Cathy became quite fond of Paul.

The whole family shared an interest in rock 'n roll music and motorbikes, and Paul used to take Cathy and her mum to dances and concerts in different towns and to stay overnight with friends.

The trouble began after Gary – the eldest boy – was born. Her mum was not well during the pregnancy and there were then babysitting problems. Gradually Cathy used to go with Paul to the dances and stay away overnight. It was then that the sexual abuse began. Threats were made about the family splitting up, and about the two boys – of whom Cathy is very fond – going into care. Later the threats became more violent.

Cathy is very full of guilt and fear – and terrified of getting pregnant. She fears her mum won't believe her if she tells her and she will be blamed for the family break-up.

Note
The details of this case have been left open in order to allow you to interpret the role for yourself. You will need to decide:

▶ how old Cathy was when the abuse started
▶ what the abuse consists of
▶ what kinds of threats are being made and how they are being made
▶ what kind of person Cathy is, and how she feels about herself.

Confidentiality

Respecting children's confidences

If children cannot trust adults to respect their confidences, and to act or intervene, except in extreme circumstances, only with their agreement, it seems most likely that many will continue not to talk about things that are worrying and hurting them, including abuse – physical, sexual and emotional.

If a child approaches an adult about abuse, the adult should of course give the child the opportunity to talk. The adult should explain in detail the possible consequences of involvement of other people and agencies, and seek the child's views. If the child is judged capable of understanding the implications, then the adult should not proceed with any action without the child's agreement (except in 'exceptional circumstances').

Similarly, if an adult observes behaviour, or physical symptoms or signs, or hears allegations from a third party that suggest abuse, they should first give the child (who can express a view) the opportunity to talk – offering to listen to the child; the approach should be non-coercive and non-leading; if it leads to any disclosure, then that information and any action should remain within the control of the child in appropriate circumstances as outlined above.

We are very concerned that the desire for 'inter agency co-operation' and 'multi-disciplinary team approaches' to child abuse can conflict with children's desire, need and right to speak in confidence to others about things that concern them.

The experience of ChildLine has demonstrated the need for children to have access to people who can listen, advise and counsel them about abuse with a clear understanding that the relationship is confidential unless the child agrees to referral or action. Using ChildLine, children retain the power to put down the receiver if they feel the confidential relationship is threatened. The service tightened up its policy on confidentiality during 1987 so that children are offered confidentiality 'unless they are in a life-threatening situation'. This is further defined, in guidance for counsellors, as follows: 'A situation is life-threatening if:

- the child is NOW physically so damaged that immediate medical treatment is necessary;
- the next time the child meets the abuser there is a very real danger of severe physical harm or death;
- during the call you (the councillor) have evidence that if the call is interrupted it may well be the abuser intending to kill or severely harm the child;
- The child sounds as if s/he is sufficiently scared that they will possibly:
  ▶ take their own life;
  ▶ take on a major new risk, eg jumping from a bedroom or attempt to run away;
  ▶ make a phone call from a highly unsafe environment (eg where there is a real risk of interruption by a dangerous abuser or a late night call from a call box).'

Further guidelines (currently under review – Summer 1988) define situations which are not life-threatening, but may be serious enough to trigger 'direct' action: 'eg there are some cases of sexual abuse which have been taking place over a long period of time and there is no reason to believe that future abuse will lead to violence'.

By 'direct' action, ChildLine means passing information to agencies with a duty to investigate – social services and the police. The guidelines emphasise that 'in all direct intervention cases, the child should be informed at each stage of what you (the counsellor) and the supervisor intend to do'.

The Children's Legal Centre believes that children's right to and need for confidential advice and counselling has been ignored by many agencies involved in investigating and seeking to prevent child abuse – including central government, local authorities, health authorities, voluntary services and other agencies. The DHSS guide *Working together* (1988) and other new guidance places an emphasis on sharing information between agencies – 'Inter-agency procedures should be brought into action at the earliest possible stage and in respect of every allegation'. There is no apparent regard for children's rights to confidentiality. The Cleveland Inquiry Report itself is indecisive on the issue: it quotes the Children's Legal Centre's concern, expressed in a submission to the Inquiry, but makes no clear recommendation, other than that 'Professionals should not make promises which cannot be kept to a child, and in the light of possible court proceedings should not promise a child that what is told in confidence can be kept in confidence'.

In our view there is not necessarily any simple connection between sharing confidential information between agencies without the consent of the subject (in many cases without the knowledge of the subject) and 'protection'.

In the particular area of child abuse, there seems to be a prevailing feeling that there is some legal obligation to pass on any information about child abuse or suspected child abuse to those agencies which do have a clear legal duty to investigate. This is not the case. One obvious motive for an adult deciding to break a child's confidence is fear that if the matter is later disclosed, they will then be held to have been in some way responsible, or in breach of a general duty of care towards the child. Many professionals (eg teachers, youth workers etc) seem confused about their legal duties, and advice from central government (and from local government employers) has done little to remove the confusion. The 1984 Court of Appeal judgement in Gillick – overturned by the House of Lords in 1985 – left many professionals with a belief that they could not even advise a young person under sixteen on any important matter without parental knowledge or consent.

There is an urgent need for revised guidance from appropriate government departments to inform the various individuals and agencies most likely to be approached by children and young people, about abuse or other important matters, of their right to advise and counsel them in absolute confidence (with the extreme exception that they must not of course give advice with the specific intention of faciliating unlawful acts).

The only agencies which, on receiving information suggesting that an abuse may have taken place, have specific duties to investigate and possibly take other action are local authority social services departments and the police.

The medical profession has no general duty to break confidences and provide information on patients to any other agency (save in very exceptional and closely defined circumstances). On the contrary, the profession is under a strict duty of confidentiality to the patient. We are concerned that the General Medical Council has advised 'if a doctor has reason for believing that a child is being physically or sexually abused, not only is it permissible for the doctor to disclose information to a third party but it is a duty of the doctor to do so'. The most detailed official advice on confidentiality and child abuse appears in an appendix to the DHSS *Guidance for doctors* (1988), quoting a statement from the joint Coordinating Committee of the UK Medical Defence Organisations: it emphasises that from their sixteenth birthday young people are in the same position as adults for the purpose of consenting to medical treatment: 'This is generally interpreted as giving, by statute, the right to confidentiality which cannot be broken without the patient's consent in the same way as if they were over the age of eighteen'. But for children under sixteen, the advice suggests that the right to confidentiality is 'qualified and not absolute'. The advice does not appear to recognise that following the judgement of the House of Lords in the Gillick case, under sixteen year olds have a right to independently consent to medical treatment if they have the necessary 'understanding and intelligence': in such cases they should be accorded patient's normal rights to confidentiality.

The General Medical Council's advice appears to amount to mandatory reporting, the introduction of which was strongly rejected in the Inter-Departmental Review of Child Care Law on the grounds that it 'might, in our opinion, be counter-productive and increase the risks to children overall, first by weakening the individual professional's sense of personal responsibility and secondly, in casting the shadow of near automatic reporting over their work, by raising barriers between clients and their professional advisers and even between professionals concerned in the same case'.

A clinical diagnosis of 'signs consistent with sexual abuse' in a child or young person able to understand the implications is in the view of the Children's Legal Centre a confidential matter between the patient and the doctor, in the absence of any agreement from the patient that the information should be shared with others. While, as in many other medical situations, the doctor might well try hard to persuade the patient to agree to the information being shared with others, if he or she fails, then at the end of the day the information remains confidential unless there are exceptional circumstances.

This view was confirmed in the Official Solicitor's submission to the Cleveland Inquiry: 'The Official Solicitor considers that a child of that capacity (having 'sufficient understanding and intelligence' to give permission) should be told of the extent to which information of a medical finding of sexual abuse is likely to be disseminated to, for example, police and other social agencies; and of the likely consequences in terms of intervention in family life. Such a child should be entitled to say that such information should be disclosed in a limited way or not at all even though that will preclude anything other than appropriate medical care'.

In making these proposals we understand that adults who accept a confidential relationship with a child/young person who then discloses information about abuse are taking on a formidable personal responsibility. This seems to us to be an essential part of the role of individuals in welfare agencies and professions.

No amount of multi-disciplinary teamwork will substitute for an individual trusting relationship with an adult in which a child can build up the confidence to stop abuse or to seek appropriate help.

All agencies and institutions working with or liable to be approached by children and young people seeking confidential advice and counselling about abuse and other important matters should have a clear policy on confidentiality, and a clear definition of the circumstances (if any) in which they will be prepared to breach a young client's confidence: this information should be available to the young person in advance of them seeking to use the agency's services.

Peter Newell
Rights of the child
The Children's Legal Centre

Role plays on possible sexual abuse

Time: 40 minutes

Purpose

● Rehearse situations that might be experienced and consider how you might deal with them

● Develop confidence through recognising that teachers and other professionals are already skilled in identifying children with difficulties and in supporting them

● Acknowledge the complex nature of suspected abuse, and the particular difficulties faced by teachers in dealing with such cases

● Raise awareness of the importance of liaison with other local agencies

● Identify strategies, policies and procedures of the school and local education authority

Preparation

Participants will need to have developed trust and support within the group, and be 'warmed up' before the role play.

Task

Ask people to find a partner and a space to work in. They should allocate roles, one as head teacher and one as class teacher.

Read out the situation below and ask people to role play the class teacher reporting his or her concern to the head. Together they have to decide what to do.

> **Situation**
> A small child returns from the toilet crying. When you ask her why she is crying she says her bottom hurts her when she wees. You've noticed that the child has become withdrawn over the last weeks.

Allow 5-10 minutes for the role play and call a plenary session.

Ask pairs to report on:

▶ whether they decided there were grounds for suspicion. What combination of factors and feelings made them suspicious?

▶ how would they deal with the situation immediately. There will be a range of responses to this. Some will suggest contacting the parent; others might want to talk to the education welfare officer, school nurse or health visitor, etc.

Ask pairs to role play the next step that they have decided on. For example, taking the roles of head and parent, or head and health visitor.

Debriefing
Allow 5-10 minutes for this, and call another plenary session.

Debrief the role plays by asking for comments on:

● the feelings people had about their roles

● the skills they felt they needed to handle the situation – these should be noted on the flip chart

● the information they need to fulfil their role – again this can be noted on the flip chart

● the implications for school policy

● the implications for how teachers follow LEA procedures.

Follow-up

You may want to set up small groups to discuss the development of school policies for child abuse. The worksheet/discussion prompts overleaf can be given to groups to work through. Alternatively you could incorporate the issues raised in the worksheets in your debriefing of the role plays.

This exercise will raise issues about consultation, liaison and referral with other agencies. It is, therefore, important to plan to follow it up by involving visitors from such agencies on your course (see Section 5).

Developing a school policy in response to child abuse

1 Handling the immediate situation

Discuss what you feel to be the best way of handling a situation where you suspect a child is being abused.

- What approaches would cause the least distress/embarrassment for the child?
- What might the child feel about the abuse being discovered?
- What actions/responses should be avoided?
- Where and how might further questions be asked of the child?
- What words might be used to reassure the child as to what is going to be done?

2 Managing the family contact

- Who would be the person to contact the family?
- What kind of reactions might that person expect to meet from the family?
- What kind of response will the person making the contact have to manage within themselves?
- What kind of support within the school will that person need, when handling such a stressful situation?
- Does the staff need someone or some structure for providing this support and advice?

3 Records

- What is the present policy with regard to recording suspected abuse?
- Is the present system adequate – common amongst all teachers, followed by all, monitored?
- What is the quality of these records? Are they written soon after an event? Do they include details, times, dates, witnesses? Do they distinguish between hearsay, gossip and observation?
- Who is given access to such records? Should information about 'at risk' children

be shared amongst all teachers?
- Are parents told if any record is being kept? What are the implications of telling them? Of not telling them?
- What understandings/agreements are there amongst staff about the issue of confidentiality?
- What improvements/modifications might be made to the present system of keeping records?

4 Vigilance

- How might a sensitive check be kept on children thought to be at risk?
- What are the likely feelings and anxieties of a child who knows that his or her welfare is being monitored?
- What sort of things would you want staff to be especially vigilant about?
- What would be the most appropriate way of making enquiries in the child's home?
- Who might be the most appropriate person to make such inquiries? (Head, classteacher, school nurse, community teacher worker?)
- What might be the advantages and disadvantages attached to each of these?
- What might be the likely reaction by parents to such enquiries?
- What sort of back-up might be needed for the person designated to make enquiries?
- If the child who you suspect has been abused has siblings in the same school, what should staff try and avoid doing? And what should they do?

5 Support for teachers and parents

- How could staff organise a consultation and support structure for themselves for responding to, and handling, child abuse situations?
- What could be offered by staff to parents who have difficulty in managing their relationships with their children?

Case studies

Time: 20-30 minutes

Purpose

- Explore people's feelings about what does and does not constitute child sexual abuse
- Raise awareness of the need to consult and liaise with other local agencies
- Explore the school's relationship with parents and the community and how this is affected by child abuse

Preparation

You will need copies of the case studies for small groups, overleaf. You can either give each group all the cases, or distribute individual cases around the small groups.

Task

Ask participants to work in groups of four to six. They should discuss each case study using the questions below – these can be written on the flip chart.

▶ Do you consider that this case constitutes child sexual abuse? Why? / Why not?
▶ How should the teacher respond to this case?

Allow groups around 10 minutes discussion for each case study.

Then call a plenary session and ask groups to report back their feelings and discussions about the case studies.

You may need to prompt discussion around the following questions:

▶ Did you assume that the child was black or white? If you change the colour of the child does this make a difference to your views of the case?
▶ What difference does the age of the child make to your views?
▶ What difference does the sex of the child make?
▶ Where could you turn for additional advice or support?

Follow up

You may want to follow this up by asking teachers to consider the development of a school policy for abuse using the discussion prompts given in the previous activity (*Role plays on possible sexual abuse*).

It would also be useful to plan to invite workers from other local agencies to your group as a follow up to this exercise.

Case studies

Rajinder and Sukdev

When Rajinder and Sukdev are walking home from school they often witness a local resident exposing himself in his front garden. Many children from the school have also seen this. Rajinder tells her form teacher.

Stephen

Stephen was waiting to meet his mother after school. She was late. A man and a woman pulled up in a car and suggested that they take Stephen home after they have taken him to see a puppet show at the local fair. Stephen declined the offer but tells his mother who reports it to his teacher.

Sharon

After a series of lessons in school on 'assertiveness' and 'learning to say no' Sharon discloses to you that an uncle who has been 'babysitting' has been going into the bedroom on several pretexts and has been touching and fondling her. She doesn't like keeping it a secret, but has promised her uncle not to tell anyone.

Mumtaz

A group of boys have persistently been terrorising Mumtaz in their year group. The girl is in a remedial group and several of the boys are in the same group. The teacher comes across a note written by the boys which is both threatening and obscene. It is clear from the note that the boys have had access to pornographic videos.

Donna

Donna's behaviour has deteriorated in recent months. She is often absent from school and the teacher has noticed that her personal hygiene is lacking. She refuses to change for gym and girls in her class have begun to call her names. She doesn't appear to have any friends. The teacher knows that Donna's father is unemployed and that her mother is struggling to make 'ends meet', even though she has a part-time job.

Susan

Susan is a very confident adolescent who is able to fend for herself whilst both parents are at work. She gets home from school thirty minutes before her mother arrives back. She hasn't told her parents, but during the last three weeks she has been receiving obscene phone calls. One day at the end of afternoon school she hangs around, clearly distressed, and tells you. She thinks it's another pupil from the school because of references made in the phone calls.

Adolescence?

Whilst on playground duty a young teacher sees a group of second year boys giggling and laughing in an embarrassed way. She wanders over towards the group and sees 'girlie and soft porn' magazines being passed around.

David

David is a pleasant eleven year old boy, with lots of friends. For the last two weeks or so he has become rather aggressive in class. Three girls have all complained to the form teacher that he has been making 'rude' suggestions and remarking on their bodies.

Miriam and Belinda

Miriam and Belinda have been on the 'at risk register' since the father was charged with assault. Belinda is a very withdrawn child who has had confrontations with male members of staff. Miriam develops a very close relationship with her form teacher and intimates that her sister is often woken up in the middle of the night by her father and taken on to the landing for a 'telling off'.

Marcus and Leroy

Marcus and Leroy aged nine years and eleven years have a regular babysitter as their mother does a late shift at work. Whilst getting the children ready for bed he insists that he supervises their bath which they don't like. He is very affectionate and insists on getting them dry, dressing them and tucking them up in bed.

In an English lesson on likes and dislikes, good and bad feelings, Marcus has described his bath time, which he says he hates.

Paul

In the course of a piece of writing about home, Paul (age 13) who has been living with his mother and younger brother (age 6) since the death of his father a year ago, indicates that he is having nightmares and frequently goes to his mother's room in the middle of the night. His class teacher, having identified this information, talks to Paul and it appears that when he goes to his mother's room he usually gets into her bed and spends the rest of the night in her bed. He has talked of cuddling up to her and falling asleep with her arms around him.

The mother and children have recently moved into the area and the children only started at the current school at the beginning of term, a few weeks ago. As a result, the headteacher has only met the mother when she admitted the children and the class teacher has only met the mother casually at the school gate.

This section deals primarily with the role of the relevant agencies in child abuse cases, and particularly with teachers' relationships with workers from those agencies. We strongly recommend that the activities in this section be done together with the relevant local professionals, in order to facilitate the exchange of information and expertise, and the development of professional relationships. In our experience the agencies are usually delighted to get involved, but will need some briefing on the way that school staff see the issues, and on your approach to training.

The activities in the previous sections will have raised a number of questions and concerns that teachers will need to discuss with other professionals. If other professionals are brought in at this stage in a course you will have been able to ensure that the course meets the needs of teachers participating in it.

If a range of professionals are present throughout a course then it will not deal specifically with teachers' needs, although of course it may well cover similar ground.

Visitors from relevant agencies

The first exercise in this section is a visitor exercise, in order to invite professionals from a range of agencies to join a course for teachers, and to respond to teachers' concerns. This activity allows the participants on a course to set the agenda of issues to be addressed.

Signs and symptoms

We have found that teachers are often anxious to be given a list of signs and symptoms of abuse, to aid them in detection. Other professions are often reluctant to supply such a list, because they fear that it can be so easily misinterpreted. We have included an activity on signs and symptoms that attempts to examine these issues. This activity encourages people to adopt a questioning stance to the usual checklists of signs and symptoms. It enables them to recognise that each case will be different, and that many of the signs listed by relevant professionals contain value-laden assumptions and are by no means straightforward facts. The feelings aroused by this activity will relate mainly to the professional responsibilities of teachers, and to their relationships with other professionals. It is therefore valuable to do this exercise as a follow up to the visitor activity while the visitors are still with the group. This will enable the different perspectives to be shared.

Procedures

We have included in this section another range of case-studies of possible abuse. In these the issues raised concern the point at which teachers' should invoke their local guidelines and procedures. Again, if teachers have fears and doubts about these procedures, which have been uncovered by the use of activities in Section 4, it will be helpful to discuss the case-studies with the visitors to the course, and to see how they respond to them.

Visitors from relevant agencies

 ime: 1 hour at least

 urpose

- Develop relationships with professionals from relevant local agencies
- Explore perceptions on the roles of all the agencies
- Discuss teachers' and/or parents' concerns about action taken by other agencies once a school has reported a suspected case of child abuse

Preparation

For this activity, you will need to invite professionals from local agencies involved in child protection to discuss with teachers and/or parents their concerns about child abuse. Course participants will need to have explored their values, attitudes and feelings about child abuse so that they are able to set their own agenda of questions and concerns for the visitors.

You will need to have arranged for the visitors to come, and to have briefed them as to their role in the session – i.e. that a lecture or talk is not required. You should also plan to brief the visitor about the course and the group while course participants prepare their questions. You should invite workers from all the appropriate local agencies. These are likely to include:

▶ Social services
▶ Education
▶ Health
▶ Police
▶ NSPCC.

Task

Take the visitors to a separate room or separate area of the room and brief them while participants prepare their questions.

Ask participants to work in groups of four to eight people. Allocate one visitor to each group, to be collected by the group once they are ready.

Ask the group to prepare questions to ask their visitor. They should also consider who will collect the visitor, and how introductions will be made. Suggest that they think of a sequence in which to ask their questions, and allocate questions to each group member. The questions should allow a general discussion of the issues that concern the group.

Allow 15 minutes or so for this stage.

Once the visitor has been collected the group should have at least 20-30 minutes discussion with them.

Then call a plenary session. Ask each group to comment on the main points raised in their discussions. You should then ask each visitor whether they would like to make any comments.

Follow up

If possible, plan to follow up this exercise with an activity done jointly with the visitors. This can enable co-operative sharing of perceptions and expertise, and facilitate the development of working relationships between the agencies. The next activity, *Signs and symptoms* , could be used for this purpose.

You may also want to give out some background information on the roles of teachers at case conferences, which in our experience is a question which often arises when thinking about cooperation with other agencies. A background paper is provided on the following page.

Child abuse case conference

What is a child abuse case conference?
When a child or children have been abused, or are at significant risk of being abused, a case conference is called to establish a multidisciplinary view about the incident(s) and risks.

What is the purpose of a conference?
It is to share information and to formulate an agreed plan of management and treatment, with the child's safety and welfare as the paramount aim. Within this there are five basic tasks:

▶ to share information about family history and current circumstances;
▶ to form a view about the type and level of abuse and assess the level of risk;
▶ to agree a child protection plan and to allocate roles and responsibilities within this;
▶ to make a decision about registration and to nominate a keyworker (usually a social worker);
▶ to decide on how and when to review the protection plan.

Although the conference cannot tell other agencies what to do, it will make recommendations. If individuals attending disagree with the recommendations they should say so clearly at the conference, and if necessary ask for their dissent to be recorded. If employing authorities cannot implement the recommendations, or wish to overturn them, it should be an expectation that the case conference will be reconvened.

The social services department will have to decide whether there is sufficient information for them to take legal action to remove the child from the care of its parents – called care proceedings. If there is, the case conference will need to decide whether this action is the best thing to do for the child, but the social services, as the statutory agency, actually makes the decision whether to implement this.

Likewise, the police will also need to decide whether there are grounds to take action against the perpetrator of the abuse, and it would be usual for the case conference to express a view about this vis a vis the interests of the child. The police have the options of taking no further action, giving a formal caution or prosecution.

Who is invited to attend?
The case conference brings together those who have been involved in investigating the abuse, those with background knowledge of the children and the family, and those who may be needed to help with any action in the future. There will also be a chairperson to help this group work together, and, usually, a child abuse adviser.

Child abuse is always investigated by social workers who are legally empowered to act to safeguard the child. The police can also be involved in investigating abuse and the sort of situation where the abuse is of a more serious nature, or where there is no explanation for a child's injuries, or where the explanation does not fit. A medical practitioner (usually a GP, school doctor, casualty doctor, orthopaedist or paediatrician) will also have been involved in diagnosing the injury and advising the extent to which the explanation given for it is consistent.

Those involved in giving background information will include social workers, teachers and educational psychologists, GP and health visitor, nursery staff, etc.

All the above mentioned may also be involved in future work with the child and the family, but the conference may also invite more specialised resources, such as a residential family centre.

How can the teacher help?
The school representative may have uniquely intimate knowledge of the child. They will be able to share information about differences they have noted in the child's behaviour, for example whether she/he is happier or sadder when a particular family member is at home, whether he/she is more relaxed in care than before, whether he/she

is more pleased to come to school than to go home, etc. This sort of information can provide information about how the child views and experiences life.

The school representative will also be able to give some indication about whether care of the child is improving or deteriorating. Indications of this can include aspects of the child's physical care, such as standards of cleanliness and clothing, and also information about parental involvement, for example, collecting the child. In some cases a child may have begun to tell their teacher about their family. Sometimes the significance of remarks made by the child gain significance in the light of other information.

The school representative will also be able to help those at the conference understand what it is like to experience the child first-hand. On the one hand the child may be viewed as provocative in their behaviour and experienced as a handful. On the other hand the child may be thought to be over compliant and excessively reserved.

School may also have first hand experience of the parents. Here it is especially important to separate gossip and hearsay from factual first hand information. The objective is always to help assess the parent's ability to provide satisfactory care and protection for their child.

The child abuse register
Every local authority area has a child abuse register which contains the names of children who have been abused or who are considered to be at serious risk of abuse. A child can only be registered by a case conference.

The purpose of the child abuse register is:

▶ to provide a central reference point for information
▶ to collate enquiries to the register
▶ to ensure that there is a regular review
▶ to provide statistical data

▶ an agreed professional statement of concern
▶ a therapeutic instrument with parents (a reminder of responsibility, a target for change).

The DHSS document 'Child abuse – working together' recommends that the register is renamed 'The child protection register' and that a child's name only be placed on this if a case conference assesses that the child is at future risk of abuse and that this is accompanied by a child protection plan designed to monitor and treat the cause of the abuse. If this idea becomes endorsed it is likely that the children will only remain registered whilst they are both deemed to be at risk and subject to a child protection plan.

The appointment of the keyworker
The keyworker should be from the agency with child care responsibility (i.e. a social worker) and has the following tasks:

▶ a focal point for communication and information from other agencies
▶ to co-ordinate inter-agency activity
▶ to ensure that the action plan is regularly reviewed.

The keyworker is therefore responsible for ensuring that tasks are carried out, but another professional may be working more intensely with the family.

The child protection review
This review has the following purposes:

▶ to review the working of the child protection plan
▶ to ensure that the child's welfare and safety is ensured
▶ to assess change by examining problems previously identified
▶ to reaffirm objectives or to discuss alternatives
▶ to maintain co-operation between the agencies.

Mike Shire
NSPCC, Coventry

Signs and symptoms

ime: 35-40 minutes

We recommend that this exercise is done together with other relevant professionals in order that perceptions can be shared and relationships developed.

Note: The detection of child abuse in children who are mentally or physically handicapped, or who have special needs, raises particular difficulties which are beyond the scope of this handbook.

urpose

- Raise awareness of some of the 'signs and symptoms' of child abuse
- Raise awareness of the difficulty of interpreting some of the signs and symptoms
- Share expertise of communicating with children and parents
- Develop teachers' confidence in their abilities to know and understand the children they work with

reparation

You will need to make copies of the list of signs and symptoms on the following page. You will need enough copies to give one between two participants.

Please note that we have dealt with sexual abuse of children as a separate category and that a background paper for this is included with activity 17.

ask

Ask participants to work in pairs, and to find a space to work in. Give each pair a copy of the signs and symptoms list and ask them to complete the following task.

First, for each type of abuse listed describe one child who displays five or more of the signs and

is not being abused. Then, for each type of abuse listed describe one child who displays three or more of the signs and *is* being abused.

Participants can describe children known to them, or if they prefer, invent the cases.

Allow 20-25 minutes for this.

Debriefing
Call a plenary session and ask people what they have learnt about the use of checklists to aid detection of child abuse.

You may need to reassure participants that uncertainty about abuse is a reality, even if it is uncomfortable. The next activity, *Procedures*, will be a useful follow up because it will allow participants to focus on what they can and should do in cases where abuse is suspected.

This discussion of signs and symptoms will highlight the high level of expertise that teachers have in knowing, understanding and communicating with children. This is a factor often unrecognised by other agencies involved in child abuse, and may need pointing out.

Further reading

A short background paper on page 54, sums up some of the major signs and symptoms.

You may also want to get copies of the article by Howard Sharron *Parent and abuse* and of recent submissions to official inquiries by the Family Rights Group, which discuss the implications of misdiagnosis of signs and symptoms for parents and children. Details are provided in the Resources section.

Signs and symptoms

Signs of physical abuse

- unexplained injuries or burns, particularly if they are recurrent
- improbable excuses given to explain injuries
- refusal to discuss injuries
- untreated injuries
- admission of punishment which appears excessive
- bald patches
- withdrawal from physical contact
- arms and legs kept covered in hot weather
- fear of returning home
- fear of medical help
- self-destructive tendencies
- aggression towards others
- running away

Signs of emotional abuse

- physical, mental and emotional development lags
- admission of punishment which appears excessive
- over-reaction to mistakes
- continual self-deprecation
- sudden speech disorders
- fear of new situations
- inappropriate emotional responses to painful situations
- neurotic behaviour (for example rocking, hair-twisting, thumb-sucking)
- self-mutilation
- fear of parents being contacted
- extremes of passivity or aggression
- drug/solvent abuse
- running away
- compulsive stealing, scavenging

Neglect

- constant hunger
- poor personal hygiene
- constant tiredness
- poor state of clothing
- emaciation
- frequent lateness or non-attendance at school
- untreated medical problems
- destructive tendencies
- low self-esteem
- neurotic behaviour
- no social relationships
- running away
- compulsive stealing or scavenging

Detecting physical child abuse

Abuse covers not only acts of commission of violence but also acts of omission on the part of parents or carers. Abuse can be both active and passive.

Although environmental factors, such as poverty, unemployment or inadequate housing, should not be under-estimated, child abuse rarely, if ever, occurs solely as a result of material stresses. Parents who are socially isolated and/or isolated from their families are vulnerable, particularly those who have experienced deprivation in their own childhoods. Other factors may contribute to the risk of abuse such as marital strife, early, unwanted or abnormal pregnancies, psychiatric illness, and alcohol or drug dependency.

The school may be the first to see a child's injuries. There are a number of injuries which should be regarded with suspicion and may indicate a non-accidental cause, and these include:

▶ bruises and abrasions around the face, particularly in young children

▶ damage or injury around the mouth

▶ bi-lateral injuries such as two black eyes

▶ fingertip bruising, for example, to the front or back of the chest, suggesting shaking or heavy grabbing

▶ bite marks

▶ burns and/or scalds, taking note particularly of the type and spread of the injury

▶ fractures in children under two years of age

▶ weals suggesting beatings

▶ injuries to the genital area.

A suspicious injury needs to be accounted for. The timing, the site, the spread of the injury, the age and mobility of the child must be compatible with the history given. If the injury suggests a physical chastisement, question whether it is appropriate or reasonable, taking account of the child's age. Inadequate, inconsistent, or excessively plausible explanations, or a delay in seeking treatment for the child, should arouse suspicion.

Physical neglect is often characterised by the child being underweight, small in stature, with a poor physique and dry wrinkled skin. The care of physically neglected children is usually poor and so they may appear unwashed, unkempt and inadequately fed. This picture may become more apparent over a period of time.

Emotional neglect can also include symptoms of physical neglect but there is not necessarily an overlap. The child can be clean and physically cared for but still be emotionally neglected. Such children are frequently underweight, lethargic, and may be withdrawn or, alternately, attention seeking. Developmental milestones are often retarded and older children may under-achieve. Hands and feet may be red/blue and appear cold. The parents' attitude to the child may be characterised by a coldness, hostility, disinterest, the child failing to please the parents in a number of ways, or the parents' expectations tending to be excessive and unrealistic.

Another common form of neglect is leaving children unattended, which can have both physical and emotional consequences.

Mike Shire
NSPCC, Coventry

Procedures

Time: 1 hour

Teachers are frequently concerned about when they should involve their local guidelines and procedures. This activity allows teachers to debate different levels of response to a variety of case-studies.

We recommend that this exercise is done together with the relevant professionals from other agencies in order that teacher's doubts and uncertainties about procedures can be explored.

Purpose

• Debate appropriate levels of response to cases of possible abuse
• Become familiar with the implications of the different levels of response for relationships with other agencies
• Understand the roles and responsibilities of school staff in relation to child abuse

Preparation

Participants will need to be familiar with issues surrounding the detection of abuse. We recommend that you use the previous activity 'Signs and symptoms' before using this activity.

You will need to make copies of the case examples and the description of procedures (see the following pages) to give one to each individual.

Task

Ask participants to work in groups of four to five people.

Give each person the case examples and the description of procedures, and ask them to work through the case examples individually. Allow 15-20 minutes.

Then ask individuals to compare their results with the other members of their group. Allow 15-20 minutes.

Then ask groups to take one example of each level of response (emergency, high suspicion, low suspicion) and draw a flow chart showing the steps that will be taken within the school starting with the teacher. Allow 10-15 minutes.

Call a plenary session and ask for comments on the exercise.
▶ What factors influenced people's responses?
▶ What are the implications for schools?
▶ How can schools ensure that staff, parents and pupils are familiar with child abuse procedures?

Follow up

You may want to follow this activity up by using the checklist of questions for developing a school policy from Activity 9 .

Alternatively, you could ask each of the professionals present to describe what their involvement could be in any of the cases discussed.

Background reading

It will be important to have copies of any local guidelines and procedures so that participants can refer to these if they are not already familiar with them.

Case examples

The following are some short case examples where child abuse may be a possibility. Consider what rating you, as an individual teacher, would give to each example. When you have completed this share your ratings within the group.

	Emergency	High suspicion	Low suspicion
●When **Alan**, aged seven, changes for PE he is seen to have what looks like cigarette burns on his left buttock and chest.	☐	☐	☐
●**Marilyn**, aged thirteen, says her father shook her violently and banged her head against a wall for being out late last night. She has complained of feeling sick.	☐	☐	☐
●**Joby**, aged twelve, has come to school with his left eye black with bruising and a bruise to his right cheek. He says he fell over on the field coming to school.	☐	☐	☐
●**Helen**, aged eleven, has red marks and weals on her lower back and bottom. She says her mother slapped her for stealing. You have suspected her of stealing within school and believe that her mother is a victim of matrimonial violence.	☐	☐	☐
●**Michael**, aged six, has a number of bruises of different colours on his shins and arms some of which seem like fingertip bruising. You have commented on this to mum before and she has denied any knowledge of their cause, casually brushing the matter aside. You are aware that Michael is one of four children aged 4 to 10. When you've asked Michael about it he has referred to mum shouting at them for being naughty and noisy.	☐	☐	☐
●**Nigel**, aged eight, repeatedly comes to school late and frequently stinks of stale urine. He seems a friendless, nervy child.	☐	☐	☐
●**James**, aged twelve, has always seemed a deprived but reasonably cheerful child. He is well known to SSD who say the family is hopeless to work with and they've ceased involvement because of this. Recently James has become withdrawn and sullen.	☐	☐	☐
●**Wayne**, aged six, seems thin and pale and appears to be losing weight. He never speaks of home and seems generally disinterested.	☐	☐	☐
●**Claire**, aged thirteen, has been arriving at school later and later and her attendance has been worse since the start of the new school year.	☐	☐	☐
●**Jackie** is aged thirteen. You are her new English teacher and this morning she told you that her parents were out all last night drinking and that this happens regularly. You know there are three younger children, the youngest being an eighteen month old toddler.	☐	☐	☐
●**Darren** is twelve. He has a younger brother and sister aged eight and five. It is well known that his parents are certified drug addicts. Today, Darren has seemed unusually vague and drowsy.	☐	☐	☐
●**Paul and Debbie** are respectively eight and six. Their father is a well known chronic alcoholic. Today Paul has said that mum's gone into the psychiatric hospital and dad's come back to live with them.	☐	☐	☐

Procedures

Every local authority has an Area Review Committee made up of representatives from a broad spectrum of agencies and departments who have a direct or indirect responsibility for promoting children's welfare. These include education, housing, and social services departments, NSPCC, medical disciplines, probation service, police, local authority solicitor and magistrates. This umbrella body has the responsibility for formulating policies and practice in response to child abuse. Each Area Review Committee issues a set of procedures and guidelines on the detection and initial management of child abuse, and teaching staff and other practitioners should be aware of these. The guidelines will recommend steps which should be taken in response to the detection or disclosure of abuse. Broadly speaking there are three levels of response which relate to the level of suspicion or certainty that a child has been abused, combined with the level of risk that the child is felt to be at. The initial assessment the school comes to will dictate the level of response.

The three levels of response are emergency, high suspicion and low suspicion.

Emergency

This level of response is concerned with the child who has a serious injury or who is believed by the school to be in serious danger of abuse or further abuse if he or she returns home. This situation is quite rare and would invariably apply to a child who has been seriously attacked by their parents or abused in some other way that puts their life in danger.

What to do

Ensure prompt medical attention. Where a child has been seriously injured this would normally be at a local accident or casualty hospital.

Secure the child's safety. Note that the social services department, the NSPCC and the police can obtain a Place of Safety Order if the child is endangered.

Ensure the abuse is investigated. Investigations into abuse are undertaken by social workers in the social services department and the NSPCC. Consider whether the case is sufficiently serious to be referred directly to the police for investigation.

Inform the parents. Normally, all reasonable efforts must be made to contact the parents to inform them of the action taken and to invite their co-operation and participation in the enquiries. Consider who would normally inform the parents – the school or social worker? If the parents are unavailable or withhold their consent to the child's medical treatment a member of the school staff can act *in loco parentis* and should accompany the child.

High suspicion

This relates to a child who the school believes may have been injured or abused by their parents but who is apparently in no immediate danger. The evidence may suggest that the child has been abused but further investigation is needed to gauge the level of risk to the child and what further steps need to be taken, such as the child's removal to a place of safety.

Things to do

Notify the social services department who would arrange for social workers to investigate. This would normally begin with the social worker interviewing the child.

In consultation with the social services department the school should **arrange for the child to be medically examined**. Consider who might do this (for example school medical officer, school nurse, etc).

Inform the parents of the action taken and invite their cooperation and participation in

▷

the enquiries. Normally the school would inform the parents but this could be by mutual arrangement between the school and the social worker. Note that if the parents cannot be contacted or withhold their cooperation a member of the school staff can act *in loco parentis* and can accompany the child at the medical examination.

Note: The school medical officer or hospital doctor would normally have responsibility for informing the family GP.

Low suspicion

This relates to situations when parental behaviour towards their children or things the child does or says arouse suspicion, but where there is no clear evidence of physical ill treatment, neglect or other abuse.

Things to do

Consider what steps can be taken to **monitor the child** within school and over what period.

- What discussion should there be with the child?

- Are there other ways in which more information about the suspected abuse can be obtained from the child?

- Who else could advise or assist the school e.g. school medical officer, school nurse, educational psychologist.

- At what point should concern lead to consultation with or referral to social services department or NSPCC?

Mike Shire
NSPCC, Coventry

Questions

- Do you know about the child abuse procedure and guidelines. Is there a copy on the school premises and where is this held?

- Are you aware of *in loco parentis* and your school's policy in relation to operating this. Legally, schools can arrange for children to be medically examined and treated but are you aware if your school has a policy relating to this?

- If a teacher is concerned that a child may have been abused what does he or she do with this? Who does the teacher take their suspicion to? Does the teacher know what that person will do with this suspicion? In other words, does the school have any established guidelines or procedures for teachers who suspect the child is being abused?

- Who in your school has the authority to refer child abuse outside the school? Do you trust the responses of your school to child abuse. If not what can you individually do about this when faced with a particular incident?

- Do you have an identified teacher with particular responsibilities relating to child abuse? If so, are you aware of what their responsibilities are?

- Is the school aware if there is a child abuse specialist or consultant you can call upon for advice employed by either social services department or NSPCC?

- When and how should parents be informed that the school suspects their child has been abused?

- Are you aware of what social workers do when they receive a report that a child is suspected of being abused?

6 Sexuality

It is ironic that many materials which are concerned to prevent child sexual abuse do not deal with the issue of sexuality. Professionals need to come to terms with a variety of issues here – perhaps the most difficult is that they themselves may find cases of sexual abuse titillating. In addition their self image is bound up with the way they perceive sexuality. Their attitudes to the opposite sex will underly their own personal relationships. It is therefore important to provide opportunities for these issues to be explored in a trusting atmosphere, before professionals go on to develop work with children.

Images of sexuality

This activity examines media images of sexuality, including the portrayal of children. It raises issues about perceptions of sexuality, of morals, and of power relationships between men and women. It sets the context for discussion of child sexual abuse by examining conflicting values and norms about acceptable/unacceptable sexual images in the media.

Likes and dislikes of one's own sex

This activity encourages you to explore perceptions of gender, and the way it relates to your own self image.

The development of sexuality

This exercise asks you to reflect on your own childhood and adolescence in order to construct a 'time line' which illustrates your own sexual development. These time lines can then be used as the basis for discussing notions of normal sexual development. This discussion is a vital first stage before considering definitions of sexual abuse. This activity should only be used by a trusting and supportive group.

Making definitions

This activity allows a group to pool knowledge and understanding of sexual abuse in order to arrive at a definition of child sexual abuse. You can follow this exercise with work on local procedures using activities from Section 5. Participants are likely to confront their own feelings about abuse, so again, the activity should not be done before trust has developed within a group. You should also remember that some participants may have been sexually abused. In rare cases the group may include someone who has sexually abused a child.

Resources for sex education

The Resources section lists a number of books which are helpful in developing school sex education programmes. We particularly recommend the Clarity Collective's *Taught not caught*.

Images of sexuality

Time: 30-40 minutes

Purpose
- Raise awareness of media messages about sexuality
- Examine perceptions of sexuality
- Debate values and ethics about sexual images in the media

Preparation
You will need a collection of press cuttings, articles, photographs and advertisements which portray a range of images about sex and gender. For example:

▶ news items from the tabloid press

▶ 'page three' pin ups

▶ advertisements portraying children in sexual ways

▶ advertisements which show men as powerful (women as weak)

▶ advertisements using women as sex objects

Alternatively, you can provide a range of newspapers and magazines, and ask participants to find their own examples of relevant cuttings.

You will also need large sheets of paper, scissors, glue and felt tip pens.

Task
Ask participants to work in groups of four to six people. Give each group a collection of press cuttings (or newspapers and magazines), a large sheet of paper, scissors, glue and pens.

Ask each group to make a collage which makes a statement about the way sex and gender are portrayed in the media. Allow 10 to 20 minutes for this.

Call a plenary session and ask groups to present their collages.

Debriefing
Focus on:

▶ How do participants feel about the portrayal of men, women and children in the media?

▶ What have they learnt about other people's views and perceptions?

▶ What are the implications of this for thinking about child sexual abuse?

Likes and dislikes of one's own sex

*T*ime: 30-40 minutes

This activity encourages participants to explore their own feelings about gender. It requires a group with roughly equal numbers of men and women.

This activity can often result in the people expressing anger and hurt. Group leaders should be prepared to make sensitive and constructive use of this.

*P*urpose

- Raise awareness of feelings about one's own sex
- Raise awareness of feelings about the opposite sex
- Raise awareness of feelings about the opposite sex's view of one's own sex

*P*reparation

You will need flipcharts and felt tip pens.

*T*ask

Participants should work in single sex groups of about five people. Ask them to brainstorm 'What is good and bad about being one's own sex?' and 'What is good and bad about the opposite sex?'. Use flipcharts to record ideas.

You may need to remind them that the ground rule for brainstorming is that all comments should be accepted without discussion initially.

Allow around 5 to 7 minutes for this stage. Then ask groups to exchange flip charts so that a male group receives a female group's chart and vice versa. The group should discuss the statements on the chart. Allow 10 minutes or so for this discussion, and ask each group to appoint a person to report back.

Call a plenary session. Ask for reports on feelings raised by the statements made on the flip charts. Were people surprised, angry or hurt?

You may need to point out that the anger and hurt relate to a lifetime's experiences, and are not simple responses to a statement. You may also want to point out that anger can be a constructive emotion, providing motivation to work for change.

The development of sexuality

ime: 50 minutes – 1 hour

This activity asks participants to reflect on their own childhood and adolescence in order to construct a 'time line' which illustrates their increasing awareness of sexual feelings and their own sexuality. It should only be done in a trusting and supportive group.

Purpose

- Raise awareness of some of the influences on the development of individual sexuality
- Explore perceptions and understandings of the idea of 'normal' sexual development
- Explore notions and definitions of sexuality
- Set the scene for discussion of sexual abuse

Preparation

It is important that group members feel comfortable working together. They will also need to be 'warmed up' for it, so use another activity in preparation.

You will need felt pens and large pieces of paper for each participant.

Task

Hand out sheets of paper and felt pens to each participant. Ask individuals to think about their own childhood and adolescence. Then draw a 'time line'. Then ask them to identify events, feelings and relationships in their childhood and adolescence which were important in the development of their own sexual awareness – their own increasing awareness of sexual feelings and sexuality – and to mark these events on the line.

Ask them to mark both high and low points on these 'time lines'. Let them know that their time-line is to be shared with one other course member, **so they should disclose only as much as they wish**. Allow 15 to 20 minutes for this.

Ask participants to form pairs and to share their time lines. Allow another 20 minutes for this.

Reconvene the whole group and ask group members to call out key 'landmarks' of the development of their sexuality. (They need only call out landmarks that they are willing to share with the whole group). Note these landmarks on a flip chart.

Debriefing

Focus on some of the key landmarks noted by the group. What do these landmarks say about what constitutes 'normal' sexual development?

Follow up

It is useful to follow this with the next activity, *Making definitions*. This will allow participants to examine the notion of sexual abuse in the context of their own increased understanding and awareness of 'normal' sexuality.

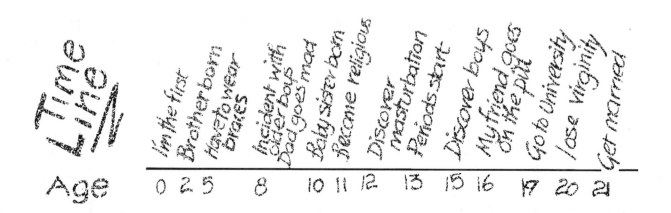

Making definitions

*T*ime: 40-50 minutes

This activity allows a group to pool their knowledge and understanding of sexual abuse in order to arrive at a definition of child sexual abuse.

In debating what constitutes sexual abuse, participants are likely to confront complex feelings about their own sexuality. Therefore this activity should not be attempted before group trust exists.

*P*urpose

- Share ideas and existing knowledge of sexual abuse
- Raise awareness of the complex nature of sexual abuse
- See child sexual abuse in the context of sexual abuse generally
- Debate moral issues arising from child sexual abuse

*T*ask

Ask participants to work in pairs and to make statements in response to the following questions (write them on a flip chart)

> ▶ What is sexual abuse?
> ▶ Who is the abused?
> ▶ Who is the abuser?

Allow 10 minutes or so for this, and then ask participants to join together in groups of six people. These groups should share their responses to the questions above, and write a definition of child sexual abuse. Allow 10 to 15 minutes for this.

Debriefing

Call a plenary session and ask each group to present their definition. Compare similarities and differences. Ask the groups about any difficulties they had in arriving at the definitions.

Follow up

Compare the definitions made by the groups with definitions found in local or national guidelines. The article which follows has been specially written for this handbook. You may prefer to use your own local guideline, or to use both and to ask participants to compare and contrast the two.

You will need to ask participants how they feel about the official definitions – many may be shocked or angry or upset and will need to express this. You may also want to point out to participants that they are likely to have learnt more by examining and pooling their existing knowledge before reading other definitions than if the other definitions had simply been handed out to them.

Follow this exercise up with activities from Section 5, in order to deal with participants' questions about how their local procedures operate in practice, and about the limits of their own responsibilities.

Further reading

On page 69 we have reproduced an article originally published in *The Guardian* which discusses some of the controversy surrounding detection and diagnosis of child sexual abuse. This may well be helpful reading for participants following discussion of definitions.

You may also want to refer participants to the book *Cry hard and swim* which is an autobiographical account of an incest survivor, and will certainly make people aware of the complexity of the issues surrounding child sexual abuse.

The legal provisions surrounding child sexual abuse are very confusing and can cause considerable concern. A useful background paper on child sexual abuse *Rights of the Child*, has been produced by the Children's Legal Centre.

The Family Rights Group have submitted a response to the Cleveland Inquiry which is critical of procedures and current legal provision. Teachers and other professionals are likely to find this reassuring and informative.

Guidelines

Definitions

The definition proposed by the DHSS in *Child abuse – working together* is: 'the involvement of dependent, developmentally immature children and young persons in sexual activities that they do not fully comprehend, to which they are unable to give informed consent and which violates social and family taboos. Sexual abuse may also include the exposure of children to sexual stimulation inappropriate to the child's age and level of development, for example pornography.'

The involvement of an adult in sexual activity with a child (a person under the age of sixteen) is a criminal offence. The type of activity and the relationship between the adult and child will determine the nature of the offence.

Referral criteria

The Area Review Committee child abuse procedures and guidelines should define the referral criteria and responses to child sexual abuse. It is helpful to distinguish between sexual abuse perpetrated by a stranger and that perpetrated by someone in an existing relationship with the child. In the case of the latter it could be a parent or sibling but it could also be a third party within the family network, for example a relative or friend who visits the child's home or whom the child visits frequently. The child abuse procedures and guidelines would normally incorporate abuse by someone in an existing relationship with the child, particularly if there is any indication or suspicion that the parents or carers have:

▶ known of the abuse and colluded with it
▶ suspected the abuse and failed to protect the child
▶ not known of the abuse but have demonstrated irresponsible negligence
▶ not believed the child or obstructed the child from disclosing the abuse in any way.

These dimensions may be indicated by the child, but are more likely to emerge during an investigation into the disclosed abuse.

In the case of abuse by a stranger it would be likely that the child abuse procedures would only be activated if any of these dimensions are suspected. A disclosure that a child has been assaulted by a stranger would normally require parents to be informed, the need for medical attention to be considered, and a straightforward referral to be made to the police.

Disclosure routes

Children tend to disclose that they are being sexually abused either purposefully, when they make a direct verbal report or accidentally, through a third party observation of play, behaviour, recognition of 'signs and symptoms', etc. This would include suspicion that a child is being sexually abused.

The child abuse procedures and guidelines will advise on how to respond to disclosures of sexual abuse. Clearly when there is a purposeful disclosure by the child, immediate action must follow as the child is in a state of crisis and, having verbally disclosed, is potentially at high risk of pressure and further abuse. When the disclosure is accidental or where there is a suspicion of abuse, observation, interpretation of signs and symptoms, gaining the confidence of the child etc., may require an extensive period of time, and the child's distress is less likely to be acute. It would seem important and appropriate for there to be close consultation and pooling of information at a multi-agency level (for example between school, social services department, police and possibly health authority) before further investigative steps are taken.

General notes

It is entirely appropriate that child sexual abuse should constitute one of the criteria for the total spectrum of child abuse and should be regarded within the child abuse definition. There are, nevertheless, some aspects of the phenomenon and of the early case management of child sexual abuse that require specific and extra consideration. This is because, first, child sexual abuse is difficult to identify and to substantiate because of the presence of elements of privacy and secrecy. There is often no physical damage (though emotional trauma may be present) and an apparently affectionate and caring relationship between the victim and the perpetrator may serve to lower professional suspicion. Often, the abuse is suspected rather than directly reported and there is a lack of clarity about who the perpetrator could be. Suspicion naturally falls upon the parent until that possibility is excluded.

In the case of purposeful disclosure there may be a specific allegation against a parent. Because of this the matter of involving or informing parents – or indeed seeking their consent to their child being interviewed and/or examined – is a particularly sensitive one in the area of child sexual abuse. Whilst the philosophy (in practice) may be to be as open and honest with parents as is possible, these ideals may have to be compromised in the interests of the child victim. Upon definite verbal disclosure the child is very much at risk from parental pressure to retract, and in the absence of any medical or physical corroboration an early parental denial may well obviate any further enquiries, leaving the child at further risk. Similarly, when sexual abuse is suspected early parental involvement would mitigate against pursuing the investigation.

Until enquiries are completed it may well be unclear whether there has been some parental culpability or collusion. Therefore, it may be necessary that the headteacher acts *in loco parentis* and gives permission for the child to be interviewed by social workers and/or police. Clearly close consultation and coordination is required between the school and these other agencies in order to resolve when and how the parents are to be informed and involved. It may be that this takes place simultaneously with arrangements for the child to be interviewed.

In these circumstances the consent of the parents to the interview can be obtained. However, if this is withheld, or parents cannot be contacted and the child is seen without parental knowledge, it is essential that the parent is advised of the steps that have been taken as soon as possible and certainly before the child is returned home. This would normally be done by a social worker or police officer.

Medical examination would normally only be indicated if it is believed that the child has been sexually abused. Because schools may be part of this arrangement it is important that they are aware of local practice in relation to who conducts this.

For example, would it be the police surgeon who is skilled in obtaining forensic evidence, or a paediatrician? What local arrangements are there for a child to be seen by a female medical practitioner?

Signs and symptoms – a closer look

We know there are lots of signs and symptoms which may indicate that a child is being sexually abused. There are many checklists available detailing these and one such is included here.

Signs of sexual abuse:

- sudden changes in behaviour or school performance
- displays of affection in a sexual way inappropriate to age
- tendency to cling or need constant reassurance
- tendency to cry easily
- regression to younger behaviour, such as thumb-sucking, playing with discarded toys, acting like a baby
- complaints of genital itching or pain
- distrust of a familiar adult, or anxiety about being left with a relative, a baby-sitter or lodger
- unexplained gifts or money
- depression and withdrawal

- apparent secrecy
- wetting, day or night
- sleep disturbances or nightmares
- chronic illnesses, especially throat infections and venereal disease
- anorexia or bulimia
- unexplained pregnancy
- fear of undressing for gym
- phobias or panic attacks

How to make sense of checklists

First of all, it is important to recognise that children who exhibit some of these signs or symptoms are not necessarily being sexually abused. Many of the symptoms which indicate that a child is upset or troubled in some way may arise from other causes. Therefore, on their own these indirect signs and symptoms do not necessarily indicate sexual abuse. In order for us to suspect that a child is being sexually abused they need to accompany or corroborate suspicion arising from a third party (eg teacher) observation of the child's play, behaviour, etc.

This play or behaviour will have a sexual aspect to it which triggers questioning on the part of the third party. For example, if a child indicates knowledge in their play or communication or behaviour which is inappropriate to their age and development, the question arises of where this level of sexual knowledge has been gained.

What is important is that an open mind should be kept with any child exhibiting a number of these symptoms or any one of them to a marked degree. Further enquiries might then alert to the possibility that the child is being sexually abused.

In the case of a child making a direct or purposeful disclosure, information subsequently gathered about the child from within the school and their home life may reveal the presence of signs and symptoms which now make sense in the light of the disclosure. However, it is important to note that not all sexually abused children will exhibit clear signs of disturbance. Some will be model pupils displaying none of the characteristic effects of sexual abuse.

Medical responses

A medical examination would normally be arranged as part of an investigation into a direct or indirect disclosure of sexual abuse only if there are physical symptoms present suggesting sexual abuse (like sexually transmitted disease or other symptoms which corroborate a disclosure) or where the investigation indicates a definite possibility that the child has been sexually abused in a way which could provide medical evidence. It is important to note that medical evidence can confirm sexual abuse. The absence of medical evidence never disproves it.

A summary

In being alert to the possibility of child sexual abuse we need to look at:

- what children say directly or indirectly
- what children do, for example, in their play, drawing, etc.
- the context for their behaviour
- any other signs or symptoms
- corroborative information?

We begin to build a picture of the child in all areas of their life. Do not let this make you press the panic button. Do let it prompt further questioning, exploration, and consultation.

**Mike Shire
NSPCC, Coventry**

The signs that point in the wrong direction

The Royal College of Psychiatrists convened a special committee earlier this year to report on professional practice and procedures relating to the field of child sexual abuse, because of the controversial diagnostic methods of some of its members. Some specialist paediatricians and radiologists have felt obliged to form a group specifically to counter allegations that their medical diagnoses of physical child abuse are frequently unsound. In April, Family Law Reports devoted a special edition to child abuse, which detailed High Court judges' misgivings about some of the methods used by some psychiatrists to get alleged victims of child abuse to disclose their suffering.

David Pithers, a child psychotherapist and leading authority on child sexual abuse, is extremely worried about the dangers of current diagnostic practice. 'What people are looking for is some kind of definitive sign. But there is terrible complexity in sexual abuse. To make a judgement on a single medical sign is simply not good enough.'

'I have seen children who have been very sore around their bottoms and abuse was suspected, but it turned out that detergent in bubble bath was the problem. There are a few but increasing number of wrong diagnoses, and it is time we did something about it. What we are talking about when a family is wrongly accused of child abuse is a tragedy of monumental proportions.'

Another trend is the failure of social workers to carry out the necessary social investigations into families before issuing traumatic place of safety orders to remove the child. This represents a collapse of social work theory and practice before medical expertise and the moral panic over child abuse.

Even if social workers did refer allegedly abused children to specialist colleagues, psychologists or psychiatrists for diagnostic interviews, the problems of interpretation would not disappear. The same trends are apparent here and the subjects of bitter controversy.

The methods promulgated by Dr Arnon Bentovim at Great Ormond Street Hospital – using anatomically correct dolls, the systemic approach to interviewing children and the principle of 'equal pressure' – are becoming the standard non-physical way of diagnosing sexual abuse. Yet lawyers and psychiatrists find that the techniques presume guilt, are highly unreliable and damaging to young children.

If, in one of Great Ormond Street's scripted, highly pressurised and very long interviews, a child straight-forwardly denies the repeated suggestions that he or she was abused, this is seen as 'blocking' because of the nature of the trauma. So 'equal pressure' is applied in the best interests of the child, to unblock them. If under pressure the child says what the adults are demanding of him or her, and then retracts it, this too is discounted because retraction is a feature of sexual abuse.

'It is difficult to appreciate the horror of the questioning technique without seeing one of the Great Ormond Street videos,' says Kim Spellar, a London lawyer who specialises in child abuse cases, and believes that three of his cases in the past year were destroyed because of mistaken diagnoses of sexual abuse.

'It is impossible for children not to become very confused and anxious, to the point that they will answer in a way the interviewer wants.'

'Children don't necessarily draw clear lines between pretence and reality and this is exploited in very stressful situations, for young children. Once in this situation, they don't stand a chance of not condemning their parents.'

A growing number of psychiatrists dissociate themselves from highly pressurised interviewing techniques. Dr Elizabeth Tylden, honorary consultant psychiatrist at University College Hospital in London, has campaigned since the fifties to get sexual abuse better recognised, but finds these methods quite horrendous: 'They keep asking leading questions,' she added, 'until they get the answers they want. I have seen two videos and both involved hard bullying of the children until they gave in.'

David Pithers believes the anatomically correct dolls are misleading and should never be used in interviews. He prefers neutral materials like plasticine, and child-centred discussions, he asks how a scripted interview – convenient for dissemination to unskilled staff – can ever be child-centred.

In six cases in 1986/7 where videos of diagnostic interviews were presented as evidence of sexual abuse, judges have been highly critical. In the case of Re V E. (a minor) for example, in March, 1986, Judge J Ewbank suggested not only that there was a presumption of guilt in the Great Ormond Street interview and that the questions would not have been permissible in court, but that the social worker's conclusions of abuse were at strange variance with the child's answers in the video and the transcript of the interview. The judge found that sexual abuse had not occurred and that the social worker's report, 'with its firm conclusions, led to a series of events which prejudiced the child and her father.'

It was also found that the mother in the case had made the allegation in an attempt to prevent the father from getting custody of the child after separation – a phenomenon which lawyers say is becoming increasingly common.

Sexual abuse of children is generally considered far more difficult to diagnose than physical abuse. But medical certainties here have also recently been challenged. Dr Colin Patterson, a bone specialist from the University of Dundee, has proved in seventeen cases in two years that so-called abuse involving broken bones was in fact various forms of brittle bone disease.

He persuaded the court to give these children back to their parents because the interpretation based on evidence by radiologists, paediatricians and social workers was unreliable and indeed went against common sense. In almost all these cases, professionals alleged that parents had battered their children and caused large numbers of fractures, yet the children had no external signs of bruising or trauma whatever.

A group of doctors, based in Leeds, has been formed to counter Dr Patterson's criticisms of their diagnostic methods.

It is hard not to lay a large part of the blame for the way moral panic about child abuse had distorted professional practice at the feet of the NSPCC, whose claims about its incidence were shown to be highly questionable in the Guardian in November, 1983. In the four years since then, it claims, child deaths caused by abuse have risen by four hundred per cent, from one to four deaths a week.

Dr Phillip Connell, a member of the Royal College of Psychiatrists' working party on child sexual abuse and a critic of the Great Ormond Street methods believes that child abuse has become an industry. Professional groups like paediatricians, radiologists, psychologists, psychiatrists and social workers have had much to gain and, in the case of the last group, much to lose. It is hard to believe that the authoritarianism, intellectual arrogance and bureaucratic ruthlessness of the welfare professionals is not an important part of the underlying problem.

Howard Sharron
The Guardian July 8 1987

Activities from the previous sections will have raised awareness of professionals' need to develop skills in supporting children who are suffering abuse, and, in particular, to develop skills in listening and responding to disclosures. This section contains a range of exercises designed for this purpose. You may have time to work through all of the exercises, or you may decide to select one or two.

Sensitive listening

These exercises develop participants' skills of sensitive listening which also allow people to rehearse possible responses to disclosures or being asked for help. You can use all or some of the exercises. In debriefing it is crucial to draw attention to the implications of the issues raised for responding to child abuse.

Sensitive responding

The second set of exercises develop responding skills, and are designed to help people develop awareness of the need to give responses which are open, and which allow the person who is talking to explore their feelings and concerns. Again, you could work through all these exercises, or select one depending on the needs of your group.

Sensitive listening

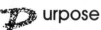ime: 30 minutes per task

Purpose

- Raise awareness of barriers to listening
- Develop listening skills
- Rehearse listening skills in preparation for disclosures which may be made in one's work

Task 1
Listening without responding

This exercise focuses on the importance of remembering details –phrases, emphasis, significant people and other factual information. Ask participants to work in pairs, and to find a space to work in.

In pairs, one person should speak to the other for 3 minutes about his/her last week or holiday in as much detail as possible, however trivial. Then reverse for 3 minutes. You will need to be strict about calling the time. Then ask the pairs to discuss what it is like to speak without interruption, and to be relieved of the responsibility of having to respond. Allow around 3 minutes for this.

Still working in pairs, now ask the person who spoke second to repeat what the first person said as accurately as possible – in the same order, and with as much detail as possible. The listener is not allowed to prompt or give assistance.

After 3 minutes reverse this.

Ask participants to discuss economy, omissions and possible reasons for these, and how it felt to listen to the 'play back'.

Call a plenary session and ask for comments. You can structure the feedback around the following questions:

▸ How did people feel?
▸ Did you/your partner's emotions interfere with your ability to listen?
▸ Are there some words or phrases that, for you, trigger a resistance to listening?
▸ Are there any topics to which you find it difficult to listen accurately?
▸ What is the significance of this for child abuse?

Alternatively, you could go round the group asking participants to complete, in turn, the statement 'I stopped listening when ....'

Task 2
Listening to the 'bass line'

This exercise focuses on non-verbal messages as well as verbal ones, and looks at the ability of the listener to understand feelings being expressed.

Ask participants to work in pairs and to find a space to work in.

In pairs, one person speaks to the other without interruption for 3 minutes, either about 'A situation I handled well' or 'A situation I handled badly' or 'My childhood'.

You will need to keep time for the group. After 3 minutes ask the listener to feed back to their partner the underlying feelings as well as the more obvious ones from both verbal and non-verbal messages. The speaker should then comment on the accuracy of this.

Then reverse the exercise.

Call the group together and ask for comments using the structure for feedback suggested for the first task above.

Task 3
Watching discussion

This exercise is similar to the previous task, but here an observer also comments on verbal and non-verbal messages.

Ask participants to form groups of three and to find a space to work in. They should take turns to be listener, responder and observer. Each speaker has 3 minutes, uninterrupted, but the listener can help with minimal encouragement. The speaker should talk about 'a time when I was very angry, upset or frightened'.

After 3 minutes the listener should feed back to the speaker the underlying and the more obvious feelings. The accuracy of these should be discussed and the observer should add comments. Continue until each person has spoken.

Call the group together and ask for feedback. Again, you can use the structure suggested above.

Sensitive responding

 ime: 30 minutes per task

 urpose

- Raise awareness of the importance of the way one responds in closing or opening avenues of conversation
- Develop skills in responding
- Rehearse responses in preparation for disclosures in the context of one's work

 ask 1

Practising responses

This exercise explores appropriate responses to a variety of statements.

 reparation

Copy the statements below onto separate cards or pieces of paper. Make copies for each pair of participants. For each pair of participants split the statements into two sets, and put the sets in envelopes. For example, put statements one to three in envelope A and statements four to six in envelope B.

Statements

1 We have heard that we have been accepted as adoptive parents for a physically handicapped child.

2 My son has been suspended from school for vandalism which he tells me he has had no part in.

3 My partner and I are going on our first holiday without the children since the first was born sixteen years ago.

4 I have recently learned that the growth which the doctors at first thought might be malignant was in fact harmless.

5 I have an interview for a job next week; although I have been short-listed twenty times so far, I've never got the job.

6 My life is a blank.

Ask participants to work in pairs and to find a space to work in. Distribute the envelopes with statements in them, so that each pair has a complete set of statements.

Each participant takes turns to read out a statement. Their partner must then respond. Following each response they should discuss:

- How the response made them feel
- Whether it facilitated or prevented further conversation
- Other possible responses and the consequences of these.

Allow around 30 minutes for this and then call the group together. Ask for feedback and comments around the following questions:

- Was a very positive response always helpful?
- How helpful is surprise? Enthusiasm?
- How important were non-verbal cues to help people make appropriate responses?

Ask participants to compile a checklist headed 'how to be a good responder'. This can be written on the flip chart, and then typed as a course handout.

 ask 2

Knowing how to respond

The following statements present some difficulty to listeners in knowing how best to respond.

Ask participants to discuss each statement in turn, working in pairs or small groups.

Statements

1 I feel like sticking a knife in my wife/husband.

2 I can't stand men/women.

3 You're not helping me at all.

4 When am I going to start feeling better?

5 I'm wasting your time. There must be people with bigger problems than me.

6 My father would kill me if he knew I'd talked to you.

Debriefing

With the whole group, focus on the kinds of responses which open up a conversation, and on those which close it down.

Again, a checklist can be compiled as suggested in task 1.

Task 3

Reflecting what has been said

In this sequence of exercises the person who is responding helps the speaker to clarify his or her own thinking, emotions, decisions and problems by 'mirroring' the content and feelings of what is being said.

Ask participants to work in pairs and to find space to work in.

Part 1

One person speaks for 3 minutes on something he or she feels strongly about. The listener helps by reflecting back feelings while the first person is speaking. Then the partner reflects to the speaker the feelings expressed using the structure:

'You felt .... because ....'

The speaker comments on the accuracy.

Part 2

Each pair of participants is given two of the four scripts, and take it in turn to speak and listen. The listener has to help the speaker by reflecting back the feelings about what is being said. Allow around 5-7 minutes per script.

Scripts

1 My life is much better now I've got my health back. Before, having six children was too much for me, but now I want to have them all at home and I'm sure I can look after them .

2 You know, it's six months since Paul was killed in an accident and I still find myself going into his room and having a quiet weep. I still miss him terribly.

3 I'm delighted with the progress I've made. Previously, just getting through the day was a real effort, and I used to dread the mornings. Now things don't upset me so much.

4 I want the landlord to do something about the damp in the flat, particularly as the baby had bronchitis last winter. Since I asked him, he still hasn't come. I'm sure he'd have done something by now if it were a man making the complaint.

Call the whole group together to debrief the exercise. Focus on ways the responses were helpful and unhelpful, and on verbal and non - verbal cues.

You can summarise the feedback by devising a checklist for responding as suggested in task 1.

8 School and classroom ethos

These activities explore the 'hidden curriculum' of the school and classroom to raise awareness of the impact that this can have on pupils. It can influence both their readiness to disclose to teachers and the messages which are transmitted about adult/child relationships. A central theme of recent publications on child abuse for schools is that they should encourage pupils to report instances of abuse, and that they should enable pupils to tell adults to stop doing something which they dislike. Yet many adult/child relationships are based on children obeying adults simply because they are adults. It is therefore vital to examine these issues if schools wish to develop preventive work on child protection.

We recommend that you use at least the opening activity *Design an uncaring school* if you want to examine strategies which schools can adopt to prevent child abuse and protect children.

Design an uncaring school

This activity raises awareness of the ways schools can make it impossible for children to disclose, and of the ways schools can reinforce traditional adult/child power relationships.

Activities to develop self esteem

The classroom ethos is as important as the ethos of the school. If pupils are to learn to value and respect themselves and others, the classroom environment must be one where pupils respect each other, and where the teacher respects them.

Moreover, it is becoming clear that one reason that children do not report abuse is not simply because they are frightened of the abuser, but also because they feel they are to blame. Such self-blaming is tied up with the self esteem of a child. A self confident child is less likely to blame him or herself, and more likely to report. We have included a number of ideas for developing self esteem. They could be used on a training course to raise awareness of the need for such work to be planned into cross curricular approaches to prevention. Where schools are confident that their personal and social education policy does support the development of children's self esteem, you could omit these activities.

However, you still might like to select one or two to use as warm-ups in the later stages of a course.

Effective parenting?

Schools are increasingly aware of the need to develop good relationships with parents. Yet many local authority child abuse procedures seem designed to widen the gap between home and school. There are several issues here. Parenting is a difficult, exhausting and undervalued job in our society. Schools can do much to support parents, and teachers need to become aware of the need to do this.

Moreover, most parents are also concerned to protect their children from abuse, and to have a trusting relationship with their children, so that their children could disclose instances of abuse to them. This means that parents as well as teachers need to look at adult/child power relationships. Teachers might consider setting up parent workshops to explore the issues being looked at in the preventive curriculum. This activity encourages them to think about the design of a parent workshop. At the same time it explores the complexity of issues raised by consideration of child-rearing, and challenges the notion that there are 'good' and 'bad' parents.

Aims for a preventive curriculum

This activity is designed to enable a group of people to reach a consensus on the aims for a school curriculum which concerns child protection and prevention of abuse. It is particularly suitable to use with the staff of one school, who can work out their aims, and then identify where in the curriculum these aims are already being met, and where there are gaps. This activity will enable teachers to see that the preventive curriculum will need to be delivered in a variety of settings: as part of health education, personal and social education, language work, literature, and religious education. It will also encourage them to debate the nature of 'prevention' and to recognise the limits of what schools can do.

Design an uncaring school

*T*ime: 30-40 minutes

*P*urpose

- Look at 'bad' practise in order to identify structural features of schools which make it difficult for children to disclose abuse and/or be believed
- Develop a check list of things that could be improved in one's own school
- Raise awareness of the need to develop a caring ethos in schools

*T*ask

Ask participants to work in groups of five to six people to design a school that is totally uncaring and closed to the needs of pupils and their parents. Allow around 15-20 minutes for this. Call the group together and share the designs.

Debriefing

Focus on the following questions:

▶ Could a child disclose instances of child abuse in such a school?
▶ Why was it easy to design the school?
▶ How important are each of the items listed in the designs?
▶ Would you do this exercise with pupils or with parents? If so, for what purpose? What would the task be?

Additional resources

Behind the scenes is a photopack produced by the Development Education Centre in Birmingham, which explores the hidden curriculum of schools and can be used by adults and young children. The accompanying booklet suggests ways of using the photographs with school-based in-service groups. Details in the Resources section.

Activities to develop self esteem

ime: 15-20 minutes for each task

The following activities can be used with adults and young people to develop self awareness and enhance people's sense of self worth, particularly through being valued by the group. Thinking about the kind of person you are, and comparing this with how others see you opens up possibilities for personal growth and development.

Purpose

- Develop self awareness
- Develop support within the group
- Develop a sense of self worth
- Raise awareness of the importance of a positive sense of self worth in the context of child abuse prevention programmes

Task 1

Positive comments

Group members will need to know each other fairly well to complete this task.

1 Ask participants to sit in a circle.

2 Give each member a large sheet of paper on which they should write their name in large letters in the middle.

3 Ask them to write down two or three things about themselves that they like. These may be physical, social, personal qualities for example 'nice eyes', 'kind' or 'confident'.

4 Ask participants to pass their sheet to the person on the right, who writes two things they like about the person named on the sheet.

NB Tell participants that comments should be unqualified and positive.

5 The sheets are then passed one place to the right, and so it continues right around the group. It is vital that all sheets are passed simultaneously.

NB During the activity, make the following points to participants:

▶ Try not to repeat what has already been said
▶ Be brave
▶ Write what you really like about the person
▶ Try to cover the whole sheet.

6 When the sheets have gone full circle, time should be allowed for people to absorb the contents. Initially, they will just want to read (note the smiling faces!). Gradually they can be encouraged to discuss their sheets, find out who wrote what, etc.

7 Ask for comments about the activity and its relevance for child abuse prevention work.

Task 2

Items in a hat

Ask each person to write a statement on a card about 'something I'm frightened of ....'or 'something I enjoy ....'
Collect the cards and ask group members to take a card out of the hat at random. Ask them to replace it if it is their own. Each person then speaks about the card they have. Tell participants that comments should be helpful, and that people should try to empathise with the person who wrote the statement.

Task 3

My name, myself

This activity can be used as a warm up, but only in a group where participants know one another.

Ask participants to work in pairs and to write their name vertically on a sheet of paper. They should then use each letter to start a word or short phrase which they feel describes them, for example:

> **H**appy
> **E**xtravagant
> **L**oveable
> **E**lpful
> **N**utty

They can ask their partner for help. If necessary they can 'cheat' by, for example using the letter as the last letter of a word, instead of the first.

Encourage positive comments and honesty. You can help by giving your own name and descriptions. Allow around 5-10 minutes to complete the task. Call a plenary session and ask each person to give their name and descriptions. Then ask for comments about the activity, and its reference to work on child protection/prevention of abuse.

7 ask 4

Get to know me

You will need to prepare sets of cards on which you write the following incomplete statements (one statement to each card). You need one set per group of five to six people.

I hope that
I am glad that
I enjoyed
I am best at
I most admire

My favourite book is
I am not confident when
My favourite place is
When I am older I will
I think that

I know
My favourite food is
A skill I possess is
I am
I can

My best subject is
I have achieved
I wish people would
I taught someone to
I see myself as

I believe that
I would like to
I looked forward to
I am good at
My favourite activity is

My favourite music is
I don't like
I am not sure about
It's great for me when
I have always wanted to

I wonder
I used to be worried about
My favourite clothes are
I would like to change
I want to be

I feel important when
I get angry when
I would like to achieve
I am getting better at
I'm not afraid to

I work best when
I like me when
I think what my friends like about me is
The best thing that happened to me was

I relax by
I find it difficult to
I feel more confident when
Something I'm really good at is

Ask participants to work in groups of five to six people, and give each group a set of cards. The cards should be placed face down in the middle. Group members take turns to pick up a card, read out and complete the statement, if they want to. If someone does not complete a statement, someone else in the group may wish to. After every member of the group has read one statement allow time for discussion before continuing with the cards.

When the groups have worked through all the statements (which will take approximately 20 minutes) call the group together and ask for comments about the activity and its reference to child abuse prevention work.

Additional resources

Two handbooks with a wealth of relevant teaching activities are: '100 ways to enhance self concept in the classroom by Caulfield and Wells and Greater expectations by Szirom and Dyson. Details are given in the Resources section.

Effective parenting?

*T*ime: 45-55 minutes

This activity has been designed to raise awareness of the needs of parents for support in their parenting role.

*P*urpose

- Enable participants to share their own experiences and anxieties about parental childrearing
- Raise awareness of the needs of parents
- Understand the complexity of issues surrounding childrearing and discipline
- Challenge easy judgements about 'good' and 'bad' parents

*P*reparation

Participants will need to have done some ice-breaking or introductory activities before doing this exercise.

*T*ask

Ask participants to work in pairs, and to find a space to work in. They should imagine that they have to plan a series of workshops for parents. The parent workshops are to consider issues of childrearing and discipline, and are aimed at helping parents to cope better with family life.

Ask pairs to think of all the issues involved in this topic. Suggest to them that it might help to share experiences with their partners. People's experience may derive from being a parent, an aunt or uncle, babysitting, being a teacher, or from their own childhoods. Allow around 20-30 minutes.

Then ask the pairs to try to make a list of headings which they hope would be discussed in the course of their planned workshops with parents. Allow 10-15 minutes. Ask pairs to join with another pair. They should explain and explore each other's headings, and the meanings behind the headings. Allow 15-20 minutes for this.

Call a plenary session and ask for comments and feedback about the exercise.

Issues

People are likely to have found the task very difficult, because they will have become aware of the complexity of the task.

Debriefing
You can focus on two issues:

▶ the role of schools, and other institutions, in supporting parents
▶ the inter-dependent and complex nature of issues around childrearing.

Aims for a preventive curriculum

Time: 1 hour or more

This activity is an adaptation of Activity 4 *Definitions* in Section 3 *Setting the scene*.

Purpose

- Develop consensus in a group while allowing each person to have a say
- Work out ideas on aims for a preventive curriculum
- See child abuse prevention as a whole school, cross-curricular approach
- Identify aims in order for the participants to see what is already being done in the curriculum and to identify the gaps

Preparation

You will need blank index cards or scraps of paper : enough for five cards per person.

Task

Ask participants to work in groups of six to eight people. Each person is given five blank index cards and asked to write one statement on each card to complete the sentence 'the preventive curriculum relating to child abuse should ....'

This takes 15-20 minutes. The statements are then collected and each person selects three cards that they agree with, but did not write themselves. Individuals then tell the other group members which cards they chose, and why.

The group may want to arrange the selected cards in a pattern, and/or to review those cards not selected. Allow around 20 minutes for this stage.

Then call the groups together and ask each to summarise their discussions.

Follow up

Ask the groups to review their aims and identify existing curricular provision. They should work out the gaps both in terms of content area and in terms of values, attitudes and skills. They should then make recommendations for ways the gaps could be filled.

You may need to prompt discussion of the following issues:

▶ the need for a planned, coordinated cross-curricular approach
▶ the need for approaches which involve pupils actively
▶ the need to provide opportunities for pupils to talk about their feelings, likes, dislikes, hopes and fears
▶ whether child abuse can be prevented.

The activity was used to devise the aims and content for this handbook. The ideas which emerged from the discussion of the cards were used as the basis from which to write the introduction. You could use this introduction as follow up reading.

If adults are to be able to help children then they need to be able to empathise with them. The most obvious way of doing this is to remind them of the child within them. We have all been children, and the memories of being a child are an important source of knowledge and expertise for adults in caring for children. For this reason the activities in this section are appropriate for parents as well as for teachers and other professionals working with children.

The activities start from people's knowledge and experience of having been children. The aim is to use this knowledge to develop understanding about the quality of relationships between adults and children that might enable children to protect themselves. You will need to be aware that these activities may cause some participants to remember an unpleasant or painful childhood experience. Make sure plenty of time is available for debriefing, and that the group understands the need to be supportive.

A caring adult

This exercise explores the different qualities of adults valued by individuals in the group when they were children. It can be used to set the scene for discussions about adults you disliked/distrusted/feared.

What is a family?

A frequent suggestion for child abuse prevention programmes is that we should teach people parenting skills in order that they can be 'good' parents. This activity encourages people to examine the myth of 'the perfect family', and recognise the stereotypes and assumptions that underlie views of families. It is worth including in a course in order to raise awareness of the need for family life education which builds on people's real experiences of real families, and encourage people to recognise diversity of family forms as a strength.

The needs of children

This activity encourages people to reflect on their childhood memories in order to reach a definition of the needs of children. Your own definition based on your own memories is much more meaningful than being given someone else's. The activity can be used to initiate discussion of the variety of ways that children's needs can be met, and of the responsibilities of different agencies and professionals for ensuring that they are met. It is useful to do with parents to raise their awareness of their own experiences of childhood, and how these have affected their own parenting style.

Viewpoints on childrearing

This activity encourages participants to debate their own values about approaches to childrearing and discipline. It enables people to recognise that the issues are complex and that there are no simple 'rights' and 'wrongs' about bringing up children.

Crimes and punishments

This exercise encourages debate about child discipline. It asks participants to consider appropriate punishments for a range of 'crimes' committed by children of varying ages. It encourages debate about attitudes to discipline, and raises awareness of the effect of different forms of discipline on adult/child relationships.

Childhood memories

This activity explores the complexities of the balance of power between adults and children. It encourages people to explore childhood memories about times when they felt they had no control over a situation, and so to recognise that it is not easy for children to simply say 'no'. It should only be done in a trusting and supportive group.

Additional resources

Two Open University packs make extensive use of people's knowledge and experience of having been children and lived in families, *Childhood* and *Family lifestyles*. Both packs can be used with adults and young people to form the basis of family education work. Details are given in the Resources section.

A caring adult

*T*ime: 30 minutes

*P*urpose

• Identify qualities valued by group members
• Think back and remember oneself as a child

*P*reparation

You will need a set of cards each with a 'quality' written on it. These could be those suggested here, or you could ask the group to compile their own list.

Qualities	
Lazy	Shy
Relaxed	Serious
Easy going	Disciplinarian
Strict	Smiling
Kind	Genuine
Compassionate	Strong
Reliable	Cuddly
Consistent	Assertive
Good listener	Aggressive
Sympathetic	Loyal
Sense of humour	Loving
Fair	Busy
Controlling	Open
Punctual	Likes you
Well dressed	Polite

*T*ask

Ask participants to work in groups of four to six people. Ask the group to draw an imaginary line which represents a continuum so that one end of the line represents 'caring', the other 'uncaring'.

CARING _____ UNCARING

Each person should take six quality cards at random. They should think about the value they placed on these qualities in their childhood, then take turns at placing the cards on the line. People should explain why they have chosen these positions for each card, and other group members can debate and discuss this. All the cards should be placed on the line.

Allow around 20 minutes.

Call the whole group together and ask for comments.

▶ What have people learned from the exercise?
▶ What is its significance for child abuse prevention?
▶ What is its significance for themselves as adults?

Alternatively you could end this activity by going round the group, asking participants to complete a sentence such as 'I learned that .... 'or 'I remembered ....' or 'In future I will ....'

What is a family?

Time: 50 minutes – 1 hour

Purpose

- Raise awareness of the variety of family forms in Britain
- Build on the experience and knowledge of group members
- Consider the implications of family diversity for ways of working with and supporting families

Preparation

You will need a set of photographs depicting a wide range of family structures. We recommend the 'What is a family' photoset– details are given in the Resources Section of this pack.

Mount the photographs on blank paper leaving space for people to write at the bottom of each picture. Display them on a table or other flat surface.

Task

Ask the group to look at the photographs and to write their names under three photographs they find interesting. Your wording is very important. Do not ask people to choose three photos they identify with, or you will be forcing personal disclosures.

Allow around 15 minutes for this. Then ask everyone to pair up with someone who has selected at least one photograph in common. The pairs should find a space to work in, take their photograph and discuss why each of them selected it. Allow around 10 minutes for this.

Call a plenary session. Ask each pair to present their photograph. Encourage questions and comments.

Debriefing

Ask the group as a whole to brainstorm the implications for working with families raised by the photographs, and then discuss these implications.

Variation

You can use nine photographs as the basis for a ranking exercise to discuss stress in families, for example, from the *What is a family* photoset by Braun and Eisenstadt (details in Resources section). The task would be to 'rank the photographs in order of the ones you consider to be the most stressful'.

The needs of children

*T*ime: 50 minutes – 1 hour

Many of us as young adults have vowed 'I'll never do that to my children'. This activity helps us to remember what we disliked; we might then be sure not to repeat it.

*P*urpose

- Make constructive use of participants' positive and negative childhood experiences
- Consider how children's needs can be met and who is responsible for meeting them

*P*reparation

It is helpful if participants know each other and have already worked together before doing this exercise, as you will ask for some personal disclosure.

*T*ask

Ask participants to work in pairs and to find a space to work in. Each person should jot down three things they liked about their childhood and three things they disliked. These are then shared with their partners.

Allow 10-15 minutes for this. Then ask participants to form into groups of six people. On sheets of flip chart paper each group should collect together their likes and dislikes. Allow around 10-15 minutes for discussion of the combined list.

Then ask the group to use their lists of likes and dislikes in order to make a statement about the needs of children. The statement can take the form of writing, drawing, a diagram or a combination of all these.

Allow 10 minutes or so. Staying in groups of six, they can then exchange statements, and may want to comment on another group's statement. Each group can send a representative with their statement to explain it, write comments, and note any possible amendments. This stage takes 5-10 minutes. The representatives then return to their groups, and report on how the statement was received and the group can make any amendments they wish.

After 5-10 minutes call a plenary session.

Ask each group to present their statement. Ask for comments about the activity.

Debriefing

Focus on the following issues:

▶ Who is responsible for ensuring that children's needs are met?
▶ Which agencies support children and parents?
▶ Would the definitions have been different if groups had been asked to define children's rights, or entitlements, rather than their needs?
▶ What are the benefits of having a 'difficult' childhood?

Further reading

You may want to have copies of the Children's Legal Centre's information sheet *Rights of the child* for participants to read following this activity. Details are in the Resources section.

Viewpoints on childrearing

Time: 40-45 minutes

Purpose

• Raise awareness of participants' own values and attitudes to childrearing and discipline
• Debate issues about childrearing and discipline
• Understand the complexity of values and attitudes involved

Preparation

You will need sets of four extreme statements about childrearing and discipline; each statement should be written on a small card. Some possible statements for you to select from are provided below. Alternatively, use statements generated from previous discussions and course sessions instead.

Task

Ask participants to work in groups of four and to find a space to work in. Each person should take one card with a statement on. They should take it in turns to discuss each statement; the holder of each card can chair the discussion of 'their' statement.

The card with the statement should be placed where all four people can see it. Each person then places a marker of some kind, like a ring or a pen, at a distance from the card to indicate how much they agree or disagree with the statement.

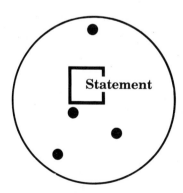

As individuals put down their markers they should explain their position to the rest of the group. Allow 25-30 minutes for discussion.

Debriefing

Call a plenary session and ask each person in turn to state something they have gained from the discussion.

Statements

1 Children are individuals in their own right. You can't force them to accept your values.

2 If you've made a principle out of something, then you must stick to it at all costs.

3 Only a totally abnormal person could contemplate really hurting their child.

4 Bringing up children forces you to recognise aspects of your character that you didn't know existed.

5 Before disciplining a step-child, a step-parent should have negotiated the ground rules with their partner.

6 Good parents needn't worry about the way their child will turn out.

7 It's only natural to want your kids to be friends with you.

8 If you have a really good relationship with your child they will want to share everything with you.

9 Children should go to bed whenever they decide that they are tired.

10 Children need a set bedtime which is kept to at all times.

11 As long as they eat something it doesn't matter what children eat.

12 It is vital to enforce a house rule that no child can have a pudding unless they have eaten all the main course.

Crimes and punishments

Time: 30-40 minutes

Purpose
- Debate what are 'crimes' of children
- Consider the appropriateness of a range of punishments
- Consider adult/child relationships
- Raise awareness of participants attitudes to discipline

Preparation

You will need copies of the 'crimes' and 'punishments' given on the next page. Provide one set for each pair of participants . You may select from those we provide, and add to them if appropriate. It helps if 'crimes' are written on different coloured cards to 'punishments'.

Task

Ask participants to work in pairs, and give each a set of the 'crimes and punishments'. Working through the list, for each crime they should select a possible punishment from those listed. If they feel none of the punishments are appropriate they can devise their own. Allow 20 minutes or so for this.

Debriefing

Call a plenary session and ask for comments on the crimes and punishments. It is important to encourage argument and debate.

Some issues to raise:

▶ Did people's feelings about crime and punishments depend on the sex and/or age of the child? Did they have to allocate a sex in order to decide on a suitable punishment?

▶ Were some punishments unacceptable in any circumstances? If so, which ones and why?

▶ Did people devise additional punishments? What were they?

▶ Were some punishments seen as ineffective? Why?

▶ Which punishments did people feel would be most effective? Why?

▶ Could some of the 'crimes' have been prevented? If so, which ones and how?

▶ What is the influence of one's own upbringing and beliefs on views about 'crime' and 'punishment'?

Recommended reading

Alice Miller's book *For your own good* provides many important insights into the effects of conventional childrearing practices on children and on adults. Details are given in the Resources section.

Crimes

1 A five year old child dirties new, clean clothes just before you're all ready to go on a family visit.

2 A seven year old child breaks a new expensive toy on the same day it was given to him.

3 An eleven year old child slips out of school and spends the day in a betting arcade.

4 A three year old child bites another child at playgroup.

5 A five year old child punches a classmate at school.

6 A six year old child regularly wets bed.

7 A four year old regularly refuses food at mealtimes.

8 A three year old refuses to use the potty and is constantly wet and dirty.

9 A four year old regularly refuses to go to sleep in the evening/night and shouts, screams and whines all night long.

10 An eighteen month old takes money out of your purse and rips up a   note that was in there.

11 A fifteen year old girl refuses to babysit for younger step-brothers and sisters.

12 A fifteen year old boy refuses to do his share of the household chores unless you're willing to pay him.

13 A seven year old child runs out into the road chasing a ball and not looking to check whether there is any traffic.

14 An eight year old steals money from your purse and denies it.

15 A nine year old is caught stealing from the local shop.

16 A seven year old does not eat the packed lunch you prepare for him every day but hides it in his drawer at school and claims to have eaten it all. You find a week's worth of mouldy sandwiches on Friday.

Punishments

A Don't speak to the child for a week.

B Don't allow the child to watch their favourite television programme.

C Slap the child hard.

D Wait for your partner to come home to beat the child.

E Use threats, for example, if you do that again you won't have any more sweets.

F Bite the child.

G Send the child to sit in a separate room for 5 minutes.

H Lock the child in a cupboard for 15 minutes.

I Ignore the 'crime' – you don't think it's that serious.

J Warn the child that if it happens again they will be punished.

K Throw whatever object you happen to have to hand at the child.

L Forbid the child from eating the next meal.

M Send the child to bed without supper.

N Don't allow the child to go out/visit friends for a week.

O Shout at the child.

P Explain firmly and calmly why you are angry with the child.

Q Storm out of the room/house yourself.

Childhood memories

*T*ime: 40-50 minutes

This activity should only be done in a group which is supportive and trusting.

*P*urpose

- Develop empathy with children's feelings of powerlessness when they experience things they don't like
- Explore what holds children back from saying 'I don't like this'

*P*reparation

You will need to make copies of the statements on the following page to give to each participant.

Participants will need to be 'warmed up' for this activity.

*T*ask

Ask participants to work individually, and to complete the worksheet. Allow 10 minutes or so for this. Then ask participants to get into pairs.

Tell each pair to talk about as much of their experiences as they feel able to, focussing on:

▶ what made them feel safe and secure

▶ what made them feel uncomfortable, unsafe and insecure.

Allow 10-15 minutes, and then ask them to focus discussion on how, in the second situation, they could have changed things to be more comfortable. How easy or difficult would this have been?

Debriefing

Allow another 10 minutes or so and then call a plenary session. Ask about issues the exercise raised in their minds about the barriers that prevent children from keeping themselves safe, or doing something about uncomfortable or unsafe situations.

You may want to prompt discussion about the following issues:

▶ Adults find it difficult to put themselves in children's shoes. This activity should help adults to empathise with children's feelings in different situations.
▶ Children have difficulties in dealing with uncomfortable situations involving adults. It's often not as simple as saying 'I don't like this and I want it to stop'.
▶ Children have difficulties in talking about uncomfortable situations.

For teachers, the exercise gets them to think about the ethos of the school and home and whether it encourages children to talk about experiences and feelings. If children aren't used to talking about their experiences and feelings in everyday life, how can they be expected to disclose difficult situations?

Childhood memories

An occasion in my childhood when I was with an adult and I felt happy and secure was ....

An occasion in my childhood when I was with an adult and I felt uncomfortable was ....

An occasion in my childhood when I felt unsafe was ....

Below we present a selection of resources with brief comments on their potential use in teaching and/or training. These comments are personal. You will need to review resources yourself before planning to use them.

Understanding child abuse

Hulme, Keri *The bone people*
Picador 1985

A novel which explores the complex and loving relationship between two adults and a 'foster' child. It is very moving and conveys the interactions and escalations in a relationship of power, violence and abuse between foster father and son. Raises awareness of the extreme difficulty of determining the 'best interests of the child'. *Recommended.*

Jones, D et al *Understanding child abuse*
Macmillan 1987

This book provides guidance on the nature and origins of child abuse and how it can be recognised. It discusses the appropriate responses for the variety of professionals who are involved. Unfortunately the book adopts a rather unquestioning stance to current knowledge about medical diagnosis and childrearing practices and it should therefore be read in conjunction with other approaches which are more critical, such as the work of Howard Sharron or Nigel Parton.

Maher, Peter (ed) *Child abuse The educational perspective*
Basil Blackwell 1987

This book contains a number of articles which aim to cover the issues of child abuse and the implications for the role of teachers in detection and prevention. There is a tendency to view abuse as something that happens to other people's children, or is done by other people. There is also naivety about the capacity of teachers and schools to change society, and some rather paternalistic views of 'good parenting'. But some of the articles provide useful background, and certainly should be read by anyone interested in examining a variety of very sound explanations.

Miller, Alice *For your own good. The roots of violence in child-rearing*
Virago 1987

Alice Miller explores the way orthodox childrearing practices encourage violence. She challenges the notion that punishment and coercion are for the 'child's own good', and illuminates the pain, suffering and long-term consequences of conventional childrearing. Her central message is that people whose integrity has not been damaged in childhood will feel no need to harm another person. *Recommended.*

Parton, N *The politics of child abuse*
Macmillan 1985

Readable background book which explores the reactions of society to child abuse cases. A variety of explanations and causes are analysed. The author shows the impossible dilemmas faced by social workers : pilloried for taking too many children into care, and pilloried for not doing enough to protect children. Clearly shows the values and ideologies underlying our approaches and responses to child abuse.

Sharron, Howard 'Parent and abuse'*New Society* 13 March 1987

Sharron discusses new medical evidence which suggests that some of the physical signs of child abuse may in fact indicate other disorders. He suggests that the current moral panic about child abuse is resulting in convictions of innocent parents. He also argues that medical knowledge about diagnosis and detection is considerably less certain than social workers often appreciate.

Spring, Jacqueline *Cry hard and swim. The story of an incest survivor*
Virago 1987

A very moving autobiographical account of the childhood and therapy of an incest survivor. Essential reading for anyone who believes that child abuse can be prevented.

Trade Union's Child Care Project *Child abuse. Final Report by Joan Lestor*
February 1987

Available from Union of Communication Workers, UCW House, Crescent Lane, London SW4 9RN

Very clearly written booklet which takes a social policy perspective in looking at key issues of definition of abuse, collection of information, and recommendations for action.

Legal and policy issues

Children's Legal Centre
The following information sheets are available from the Children's Legal Centre Ltd, 20 Compton Terrace, London N1 2UN Telephone 01 359 6251

Rights of the child

Proposals for a new United Nations Convention. A good background paper for considering the rights of children.

Child sexual abuse

Clearly written summary of the legal duties of all the relevant agencies, the law relating to child abuse and sexual assault generally, and sources of help.

Department of Health and Social Security *Child abuse – working together*
DHSS April 1986
Available from PO Box 21, Stanmore, Middlesex, HA1 1AY

A draft guide to arrangements for inter-agency cooperation for the protection of children.

Family Rights Group
6-9 Manor Gardens, Holloway Road, London N7 6LA
Telephone 01 263 4016/9724. For advice only 01 272 7308 from 9.30 to 12.30 Monday, Wednesday, Friday.

Advice on family rights and a range of useful publications which take a social policy perspective. Clearly written, the Family Rights Group papers call for the need for professionals to work in partnership with parents. The papers should be read by anyone who thinks that child abuse is something done by a few 'bad' parents. Below we list a few recent and recommended publications.

Child abuse: working together
A response to DHSS draft guide.
September 1986

Asks for a partnership of professionals and parents; the establishment of a clear, publicly known appeals procedures against case conference procedures; guidance on training and for the commitment of resources.

Inquiry into child abuse in Cleveland
October 1987

Wide ranging comment on the recent controversy in Cleveland. Considers medical evidence and parental consent, the local authority response to suspicion, case-conferences, emergency, prevention, treatment, placement, and the legal framework. Is critical of policy, law and practice and argues that children's and parents' needs and rights cannot be met in the current framework.

Tyra Henry inquiry
January 1987

Comments on: written agreements; parental participation in child abuse case conferences and reviews; skills in returning children home; racism awareness training; policing and monitoring of, and giving financial assistance to, parents and grandparents who are caring for children who are the 'legal' responsibility of the local authority.

Training resources

Development Education Centre *Behind the scenes*
DEC, Selly Oak College, Birmingham B29 6LE

A set of twenty four photographs which depict a variety of scenes in primary schools – displays, dinner time, play time, libraries, classrooms etc. Contains a booklet with ideas for how the photographs can be used in school-based in-service work to discuss hidden messages of the school. The photographs prompt discussion on issues of gender, race, power, discipline and parental involvement. *Recommended.*

Inner London Education Authority *Tom – a case of child abuse*

This 45 minute video was produced by a group of education welfare officers, teachers, social workers and medical advisors. It aims to provide a basis for discussion about the issues involved for primary schools where there is a suspicion that a child is being physically abused at home. Rather long, but extracts could be used to discuss different issues and dilemmas. However, many of the role play and case history activities in this training handbook raise the same issues and allow for more open-ended discussion. It includes materials for school-based in-service which were developed by a working group in Nottinghamshire.

Ives, Richard 'Videos on preventing child sexual assault' *Children and society* Number 1, 1987

This article analyses professionals' responses to available videos in order to give a guide to whether and how each video might be used. The author points out that video may not be the best way of approaching preventive work in any case, pointing out that it will distance and oversimplify the issues. Moreover, he suggests that much emphasis on getting children to 'say no' is misguided: *'Just saying no will only be effective in a society which makes it possible for the relatively powerless to say this in the knowledge that they will be protected if they do, or (better still) that to do so will be effective'*.

Open University, Health and Social Welfare Department *Responding to child abuse and neglect*

New course to be launched in March 1989.

This course comprises three workbooks, group exercises and a book of specially commissioned readings. It aims to provide a basic introduction to the issues. It takes a practical approach, and builds on students' existing knowledge and experience. At the same time it takes a critical approach to the literature and encourages students to examine their own values and attitudes.

Resources for personal, social and health education.

Braun, D and Eisenstadt, N *Childhood*
Open University 1985
Available from LMSO, PO Box 188, Milton Keynes MK7 6DH

A resource pack to support cross curriculum work on child development and the family. Can also be used with adult groups. Contains a variety of teaching activities and materials to explore the themes of 'Identity', 'Practical experience with young children' and 'Child, school and community.'

Braun, D and Eisenstadt, N *Family lifestyles*
Open University 1985
Available from LMSO, PO Box 188, Milton Keynes MK7 6DH

A pack containing a range of teaching activities and support materials including background readings, photocopies, and literature extracts. The activities can be used with young people and with adults to explore themes of 'What is a family?', 'Social roles', and 'Family relationships'. Designed as a flexible resource to support cross curriculum work on family education and PSE.

Braun, D and Eisenstadt, N *What is a family?*
Development Education Centre 1985
Available from DEC, Selly Oak College, Birmingham, B19 6LE
Also included in the Open University *Family lifestyles* pack.

A set of twenty-two black and white photographs depicting a wide variety of families. An accompanying booklet gives suggestions for using the photographs, which can be used with youngsters aged eight and above, and with adults. The photographs raise issues concerning values and stereotypes about family structures, roles and relationships.

The Clarity Collective *Taught not caught, strategies for sex education*
Learning Development Aids 1983

A very useful resource for those teaching family life and sex education. The activities can be used to explore sexuality, relationships, personal identity and decision making. *Recommended.*

Caulfield, J and Wells, H *100 ways to enhance self concept in the classroom*
Prentice Hall 1976

Full of practical ideas for activities to use with pupils to enhance their self esteem and develop their self confidence. Teachers will need to think about how the activities link with the curriculum they are engaged in, otherwise there is a danger that the activities will go nowhere. However, many of them are suitable for warm ups, and will be enjoyed by pupils.

Elliott, Michelle *The William Street kids: it's your right to be safe*
Andre Deutsh 1986

A series of stories dealing with a range of situations from bullying to abuse within the family. In each situation the child is given clear practical help. There is some acknowledgement that it may be hard to find an adult who will listen. Only suitable to use in the context of wider discussions about relationships and families. Children will need reassuring that real life may not always be so clear cut and it may be hard to tell.

Hopson, B and Scally, M
Lifeskills teaching programme
Numbers 1, 2 and 3
Lifeskills Associates 1987

A range of practical suggestions for group work to develop social and life skills. Useful for tutorial time and PSE.

Kidscape *Good sense defence teaching kit*

Available from Kidscape, 82 Brooks Street, London W14 1YG

Very clear, step by step teaching materials which aim to help children recognise and deal with potentially dangerous situations. There are instructions for involving parents, and very detailed lesson plans. The approach is

didactic, although fun. Put in the context of a programme of personal, social and health education the materials may be of some value in teaching personal body safety, but they do nothing to break down power relationships between adult and children in the classroom, or to challenge the view that child sexual assault can be prevented. This is unfair and unrealistic. Can rape be prevented? Should women always report a case of rape? The complexity of these questions as they relate to adults is made far more complex when one considers them in relation to children.

Kidscape also run training courses in prevention of child sexual abuse.

McNaughton, June *Fit for life*
Levels 1 and 2
Macmillan 1983

Two recent books with pupil materials on health education, for pupils aged five to twelve. Designed for pupils with moderate learning difficulties, but many activities can be used with pupils of all abilities. There are useful ideas for work on feelings and self awareness.

Rolf Harris Videos *Kids can say no* 1985
Can be hired through CFL Vision or purchased from Rolf Harris Videos, 43 Drury Lane, London WC2B 5RT. Includes teachers' notes and two books by Michelle Elliott.

Very clear, easy to follow and well-intentioned, but the

emphasis is on the child's responsibility to say 'no', or to tell an adult. Oversimplifies the issues. Can be used with parents to start discussion of the school's approach to child safety. If shown to a group of children, some of whom are suffering abuse, could do considerable harm by making them feel even more guilty, responsible and alone.

Szirom, T and Dyson S
Greater expectations. A source book for working with girls and young women.
Learning Development Aids 1986

A resource for people who are concerned to raise awareness and self esteem of the girls and young women with whom they work. It is also useful for those working with boys and men to increase their awareness of women's roles in society. Combines a wide range of teaching activities which cover values, skills and confidence. *Recommended.*

Went, D *Sex education: some guidelines for teachers*
Bell and Hyman 1983

A useful background book which teachers should find helpful in designing and planning approaches to sex education.

Notes